# POST-COMMUNISM AND THE MEDIA
# IN EASTERN EUROPE

T0347232

# Post-Communism and the Media
in Eastern Europe

*edited by*
PATRICK H. O'NEIL

FRANK CASS
LONDON • PORTLAND, OR

*First Published 1997 in Great Britain by*
FRANK CASS AND COMPANY LIMITED
Newbury House, 900 Eastern Avenue
London IG2 7HH


*and in the United States of America by*
FRANK CASS
c/o ISBS
5804 N.E. Hassalo Street, Portland, Oregon 97213-3644

Copyright © 1997 Frank Cass & Co. Ltd.


British Library Cataloguing in Publication Data

A catalogue record for this book is
available from the British Library


ISBN 0 7146 4765 9 (hardpack)
0 7146 4311 4 (paperback)


Library of Congress Cataloging-in-Publication Data

A catalog record for this book is
available from the Library of Congress


This group of studies first appeared in a Special Issue on
'Post-Communism and the Media in Eastern Europe' of
The Journal of Communist Studies and Transition Politics, Vol.12, No.4,
December 1996, published by Frank Cass & Co. Ltd.

*All rights reserved. No part of this publication may be reproduced, stored in a retrieval system
or transmitted in any form, or by any means, electronic, mechanical, photocopying, recording,
or otherwise, without the prior permission of Frank Cass and Company Limited.*

# Contents

# Introduction: Media Reform and Democratization in Eastern Europe

## PATRICK H. O'NEIL

Given the role of mass communication in the maintenance of communist authoritarianism, it is not surprising that the abandonment of censorship gave way, across the Eastern Europe, to a flourishing of the press, as new titles in unaccustomed areas burst forth. The notion of a free press is central to many models of 'democracy', and this new development was therefore warmly welcomed. However, experience in a number of countries has shown an inability on the part of the societies concerned – including the public, the politicians and the journalistic profession – to assimilate this freedom and use it in ways that sustain the establishment of democratic politics. The significance of freedom of information for the functioning of democracy is such that the development of the institution of the press and its relationship with government merits serious study.

What are the prospects for free and open media in Eastern Europe? This is a question that lacks a definite answer and is still a source of dispute. While the revolutions of 1989 were seen as a victory for liberal values over authoritarianism, in subsequent years it has become clear that the absence of communism does not alone lead to democracy by default. Rather, open societies must be built (or re-built), pulling down old state structures that served to centralize political power. Ideology and slogans may quickly vanish from the scene, but many of the organizational aspects of communism are less easily undone. The challenge is not just to replace such discredited structures, but to decide and agree on what they should be replaced with.

One of these structures is obviously the media. Under socialism, it was generally accepted that the media served as a 'transmission belt' – not from the masses to the party, in a democratic-centralist fashion, but rather from the party to the people, as an important form of control over information and society. How knowledge was disseminated and portrayed was vital for the survival of communism, stifling alternative concepts or critiques of the existing order. Indeed, the media became one of the battlegrounds of the cold war, as the USSR, its satellite states and the Western powers engaged

Patrick H. O'Neil is an assistant professor in the Department of Politics and Government at the University of Puget Sound, Tacoma, Washington, USA.

in their own propaganda campaigns over the nature of East European societies. For Western scholars themselves, the media in Eastern Europe were nothing if not Byzantine: research took the form of code-breaking, reading between the lines in order to glean and 'deconstruct' the real messages behind the distortions. Allegory and double meanings, the particular allegiance of newspapers to their party–state bosses, even the order in which the names of politicians were listed: these features were often sifted through, in a Kremlinological approach to the region that sought to make some sense out of a cryptic press.[1]

Given the role of mass communication in the maintenance of authoritarianism, it is thus not surprising that one of the most important impacts of the collapse of communism was the sudden torrent of information that burst forth. The monopoly of information gave way to a rapid and diverse expansion of the press. Newspapers and magazines appeared overnight, some emerging after years as *samizdat* publications; revelations of the crimes of the past and of national history before communism, and speculations on the future of Eastern Europe, came out of the realm of private conversation and into that of public discourse; local views, so often buried under central party rhetoric, suddenly appeared, loudly and angrily. Eastern Europe truly became an example of information overload, where the past and the present were being rewritten from day to day.

But the expansion of press freedom took place in a period of real transition, where old rules had lost their legitimacy and new ones had not yet been promulgated to take their place. Openness created cacophony, and the expansion of press diversity also created the means by which old hatreds could be publicly expressed. Real news often gave way to sensationalism, yellow journalism and tabloid coverage. Often, after the initial euphoria, many programmes or publications found they lacked a large enough audience to survive in a new system of profit and loss, and quickly folded. Foreign capital in many countries came to dominate the most important media assets, raising questions about information monopolies and external control all over again.

At the governmental level as well, the 'new democrats' were often less than thrilled with an open press. State-run television and radio have in many cases developed into the mouthpiece of new regimes, little different from their role under state socialism. Censorship laws have been resurrected as a handy tool to stifle those who criticize the government. Often, economic pressure serves the same purpose. Between market and state, the media continue to run the risk that the power over information will be reconsolidated into the hands of a few, a re-*étatisation* to the detriment of civil society.

While these issues seem a vital part of the success or failure of democracy, in Eastern Europe or elsewhere, we know little about the relationship between media reform and the formation of stable democracy. For example, in the West in recent years research on the media has grown immensely, critically investigating the concept of a 'free press' and the often negative interaction between the media and democracy.[2] These discussions are valuable and draw conclusions that are applicable in a number of different cases, but often they start with the assumption of a stable, liberal democratic order. There is general agreement among Western social scientists that democracies depend on a free press; however, studies of the inter-relationship between the media and democracy have paid little attention to how a free press forms in newly democratizing societies. Where media systems are emerging from a long period of authoritarianism, as in Eastern Europe, what impact media structures in transition have on the new political order, and vice versa, requires further investigation.[3] Here we confront an entirely different set of circumstances, which require an altogether different set of questions.

As Western studies of the media have little to say about the role of press in transitional systems, so also is it the case that those scholars who study authoritarian transitions and democratization have little to say about the media as an important political variable. Within the current study of democratization, dominant analytical approaches tend to focus upon the process of the actual transition itself, concerned primarily with the particular strategies and resources of elite actors. Actual transition events, as visible and dramatic moments, are seen as playing the critical role in the collapse of authoritarianism and the rise of democracy. Yet the result of such a focus is often that broader state and societal institutions tend to be pushed into the background in favour of a focus on the interaction of political elites.[4] There is no doubt that the role of such actors is central to the formation of democratic openings. However, beyond the transition moment, how the process of transition is sustained, consolidated and institutionalized into a stable democratic system is largely missing from such a perspective.

This exclusion extends to the media. Students of democratization often assert that a free press is one of the key 'pillars of democracy', but this idea is rarely developed any further.[5] Even where the role of the underground or opposition press is cited as an important instrument in the formation of civil society and the undermining of undemocratic regimes, there is lacking an elaboration of how open information makes the transition from the political margin to become a central element of a new democracy. Analyses of different forms of media relationships recognize that their variation depends on the particular type of political system, but these models are largely static, providing little insight into the role of the media in a changing political environment such as we find in Eastern Europe. In general, while studies of democratization recognize the importance of the media, few have gone beyond these basic assumptions to study *how* and *why* such institutions may advance or impede democratization processes.

### Rethinking State Socialism: An Institutional Approach

In the light of the dramatic changes in Eastern Europe, a re-evaluation of socialism's rise and fall may seem little more than hindsight as perfect vision. Yet there is value to be gained from it. If we proceed – as this study does – from the assumption that changes in the post-socialist period are directly connected to what has gone before them, it behooves us to reconsider the past so as to gain a better grasp of the present.

This is, in essence, an institutional approach. In contrast with elite-based views of political power, institutional arguments can be defined as studying the means by which structures and routines become self-replicating and valued for their own sake, by linking their actions to the wider social and technical environment.[6] Organizations are by nature unstable: they drift in a sea of changing social and technical relations. In order to gain greater stability and legitimacy, they often attempt to link themselves to the external social and technical environment. Depending on the terrain encountered and the opportunities and challenges involved in legitimation, this linkage may occur through a variety and mixture of forms, such as co-option, appeals to other existing institutions, licensing, or the incorporation of external norms. The environment becomes a supporting element for the organization, making the organization less dispensable to society in turn. Means and ends become blurred, often becoming one and the same.

This general process of institutionalization can be viewed across the organizational spectrum. One extreme example, however, can be found in the construction of state socialism. In this case, we see the institutionalization of the party as the actual embodiment of revolution, an end in itself rather than a means to achieve the communist goal. This is accompanied by the triumph of the institutional 'red' over the independent 'expert', eliminating the mechanisms by which objective criteria can be created to evaluate the success or failure of the organization. The institution simply 'is', and it legitimizes itself though its presumed indispensability. The greater the blurring of means and ends, the greater the inflexibility of the institution, and the greater the inability to respond to changing environmental contexts. Institutionalization thus produces stability, even legitimacy, but also ossification; carried too far, it creates the likelihood not of evolution, but increasing pressure from without, and eventually total collapse.

While the potential of institutionalization is generic across organizations, political or other, the *means* by which it takes place – that is, how organizations link themselves to the environment around them – varies widely. In Eastern Europe, how the party–states sought to establish such relations varied widely, given the different domestic conditions. Policies of technocratic rationality, nationalism, liberalization or co-option were all used in Eastern Europe as a means to build legitimacy or control or both. Socialism was institutionalized differently from state to state, from environment to environment. Thus, it also follows that when Soviet backing vanished these brittle orders all collapsed, *but in radically different ways*. In short, the process of institutionalization as it varied shaped the manner of collapse. The media in Eastern Europe are a clear example of how past institutional configurations influenced the process of media transition, shaping the contours of the present struggle in this area.

The following set of articles seeks to build upon these arguments regarding political change and paths of media reform in Eastern Europe. In order to draw larger conclusions about the interaction between media structures, the collapse of authoritarianism, and the prospects for democratization, we must gain a better grasp of the intricacies behind such cases. In Eastern Europe, we find that, although communism created a political system which was largely homogeneous in organizational terms, the role of the media in fact was distinctive in each case, reflecting the particular contours of each nation-state. Consequently, the resulting variation in transition processes was also reflected in changes in the post-communist media. How the media have fared across Eastern Europe can therefore be seen as in part a function of its position in the old order; or, as László Bruszt and David Stark have argued, how the pieces of state socialism fell apart has distinct consequences for how they are rebuilt later.[7]

These institutional legacies, for good or ill, thus continue to influence the process of media change, even as internal and external forces (such as Western think-tanks and governments) seek to reconstruct the East European media in their own image – with, not surprisingly, mixed results. By investigating the path of media change since 1989, we can gain a better sense of the interaction between information and political power during a period of regime consolidation, not just in Eastern Europe, but within authoritarian systems in general.

### NOTES

1. One of the best examples of such an approach is Jiri Valenta, *Soviet Intervention in Czechoslovakia 1968: Anatomy of a Decision* (Baltimore, MD: Johns Hopkins, 1979).
2. For example, John Keane, *The Media and Democracy* (Cambridge: Polity, 1991); Edward S. Herman and Noam Chomsky, *Manufacturing Consent: The Political Economy of the Mass Media* (New York: Pantheon Books, 1988); Judith Lichtenberg (ed.), *Democracy and the*

*Mass Media* (Cambridge: Cambridge University Press, 1990).

3.  There is developing an important literature on the role of the media in post-communist Eastern Europe. Some examples include Colin Sparks and Anna Reading, 'Understanding Media Change in East Central Europe', *Media, Culture and Society*, Vol.16 (1994), pp.243–70; Karol Jakubowicz, 'Equality for the Downtrodden, Freedom for the Free: Changing Perspectives on Social Communication in Central and Eastern Europe', *Media, Culture and Society*, Vol.16 (1994), pp.271–92; Karol Jakubowicz, 'Media Within and Without the State: Press Freedom in Eastern Europe', *Journal of Communication*, Vol.45, No.4 (Autumn 1995), pp.125–39; and Slavko Splichal, *Media Beyond Socialism* (Boulder, CO: Westview, 1994).

4.  Adam Przeworski, *Democracy and the Market: Political and Economic Reforms in Eastern Europe and Latin America* (Cambridge: Cambridge University Press, 1991); Giuseppe Di Palma, *To Craft Democracies* (Berkeley, CA: University of California Press, 1990); Guillermo O'Donnell, Philippe C. Schmitter and Laurence Whitehead (eds.), *Transitions from Authoritarian Rule*, 4 vols. (Baltimore, MD: Johns Hopkins, 1986).

5.  Larry Diamond, Juan J. Linz and Seymour Martin Lipset (eds.), *Politics in Developing Countries* (Boulder, CO: Westview, 1990); Robert A. Dahl, *Polyarchy: Participation and Opposition* (New Haven, CT: Yale University Press, 1971); Ralf Dahrendorf, 'Transitions: Economics, Politics, and Liberty', *The Washington Quarterly*, Vol.13, No. 3 (Summer 1990), pp.133–42.

6.  Philip Selznick, *TVA and the Grass Roots* (Berkeley, CA: University of California Press, 1949), and W. Richard Scott, *Organizations: Rational, Natural and Open Systems* (Englewood Cliffs, NJ: Prentice Hall, 1992, esp. Ch. 3.

7.  László Bruszt and David Stark, 'Remaking the Political Field in Hungary: From the Politics of Confrontation to the Politics of Competition', *Journal of International Affairs*, Vol.45, No.1 (Summer 1991), p.207, n.12.

# News Media Reform in Eastern Europe: A Cross-National Comparison

## ANDREW K. MILTON

Despite the euphoria in 1989–90 when solid communist censorship gave way to a vibrant press and other mass media, experience since the revolutionary period has reflected the persistence of communist and even pre-communist approaches to the collection, presentation and dissemination of news. In particular, there is a tendency for journalists to employ 'official' sources, and an expectation on the part of politicians and governments that the media will support them uncritically. In that way, it is asserted, the establishment of democracy is being advanced: by the same token, a critical press is deemed hostile to democracy as such. Legal changes have brought about significant developments in the ownership of the printed media, notably the involvement of foreign firms in ownership and distribution; the broadcasting media have been slower to change. Inevitably, therefore, institutional continuity with the communist regime is part and parcel of the reality of developing democracy, and defining the role of the media is an element in the political struggle.

> What is [the] independent life of society? The spectrum of its expressions and activities is naturally very wide. It includes everything from self-education and thinking about the world, through free creative activity and its communication to others … .
>
> – Václav Havel, 1979

There was hardly an East European communist-era reform movement that did not make some demand for reform of the media, for a free press. This was rightly believed to be a necessary condition for the creation of a democratic society: information and its free flow are central to democratic politics.[1] With such importance attached to this aspect of the changes in Eastern Europe, we must ask what kind of free press those societies are creating for themselves. This article addresses two specific questions. First, what initial assessments of news media output can we make? The current analysis finds that on two measures the media in Eastern Europe tend to rely on official sources and to under-report the 'why' and 'how' explanatory elements. The second question follows from this observation: what might

Andrew K. Milton is a doctoral candidate at the Department of Political Science in the University of Oregon, Eugene.

explain these less than desirable outcomes? In brief, I will argue that institutional legacies, left by incomplete legal reform, in which the role and valuation of the news media as an institution are carried over from the state socialist period, constrain the complete democratic re-institutionalization of the news media. In consequence, their performance has fallen short of rhetorical expectations.

In his introduction to this collection, Patrick O'Neil has already discussed the dearth of theoretical analysis about the role of the news media in democratic transitions, so in this contribution we turn to institutional analysis for a possible explanation of the news media's performance in East European societies. The theorizing about organizations (specifically, institutionalization) that emerges from the institutional literature tells us how organizations become rigid and unlikely to change, especially given the survival of institutional forms from the previous period. As this article will demonstrate, the news media's political organizational relationships and the political expectations during the communist era persist into the post-communist period. This institutional legacy has been exploited by new political actors and has generated journalistic output that is less than useful to democratic politics.

## Content Analysis

East European news media output from 1993 or early 1994 and late 1995 was analysed for the use of official sources and for the reportage of the 'who, what, where, when, why, how' elements. All the normative models of a 'free press'[2] would assert that a certain degree of diversity of sources should be exhibited, because a range of opinions and thoughts is required for the pursuit of truth and good government. Furthermore, all the elements of explanation, especially 'why' and 'how', also reflect the quality of information.

### Official Source Syndrome

In his path-breaking study of the *New York Times* and the *Washington Post* Leon Sigal found that reporters got their material from 'routine' channels (official proceedings, press conferences, and other non-spontaneous events) more than twice as much as on their own initiative (what Sigal calls 'enterprise'). Moreover, he found that American government officials or agencies (at all levels) and foreign officials and agencies accounted for over 75 per cent of the sources of information.[3] Thirteen years later, Atwater and Fico found television reporters to have an even greater tendency to rely on prearranged and predictable events for material, and to display a greater tendency to 'load up' their reports with widely-known officials.[4] The result of this reliance on officials is the skewing of the news towards the official agenda and a tendency to defer to the official viewpoint and attitude – two forms of behaviour that newly freed news media should probably avoid.

In our study, an initial assessment of the prevalence of official sources in media output for the Czech Republic and Slovakia was undertaken. These two countries were chosen for their differing historical experiences with tolerance of diversity and levels of civil society activity – the Czech Republic tending toward greater tolerance and higher levels of activity. The difference in these two factors could imply differences for media performance, so these two divergent countries have been chosen in order to get some measure of control over the influence of these political factors.

All media pieces that were reprinted in the Foreign Broadcast Information Service (FBIS) through approximately ten weeks in September–November 1993 and five weeks in late 1995 and early 1996 that covered any aspect of international relations or foreign affairs and any aspect of economic development, plans or programmes were analysed. The source of the information reported was the primary interest. Pieces that relied on official sources were disaggregated from those that used primarily independent (or 'unofficial') sources. An 'official source' is here defined as any member of the government or bureaucracy serving in a formal, recognized capacity, and 'independent source' means anything else. By this definition, 'independent' includes party leaders (assumed here to be performing a non-governmental political role), non-governmental institutions such as think-tanks, officials from other governments, and so on. These exclusions, by expanding the definition of unofficial, make 'independence' more likely, so they make for a more difficult test.

The use of official sources is further disaggregated (by a somewhat more subjective criterion) into pieces that use an official source and those that more specifically transcribe the actions or statements of the official source. A transcription is characterized by the expression, by the official source, of political preference or position on policy. Both transcription and the use of official source reflect deference, the distinction between the two being the depth to which deference can go. Interviews are counted separately, as they are another device for explicit expression by the official source.

*Czech Republic*

Out of 91 pieces reviewed from 1993, 78 relied on official sources (including 21 transcriptions and 15 interviews), and 13 on independent sources. Of the 13 pieces counted as using independent sources only six were actually independent analysis or were based on work done by the journalist. The independent sources in the remaining seven pieces included (1) the Parliamentary Agriculture Committee challenging the agriculture

TABLE 1

USE OF SOURCES: CZECH REPUBLIC AND SLOVAKIA

**CZECH REPUBLIC**

| | Official Source | | Transcription | | Interview | |
|---|---|---|---|---|---|---|
| | 1993 | 1995/96 | 1993 | 1995/96 | 1993 | 1995/96 |
| Prime Minister | 7 | 0 | 12 | 2 | 3 | 3 |
| President | 4 | 1 | 2 | 1 | 0 | 1 |
| Foreign Minister | 5 | 0 | 0 | 0 | 4 | 2 |
| Defence Minister | 2 | 1 | 1 | 1 | 3 | 1 |
| Economics Minister | 4 | 0 | 0 | 0 | 0 | 0 |
| Finance Minister | 4 | 1 | 0 | 0 | 1 | 0 |
| Other Official | 17 | 4 | 6 | 1 | 4 | 0 |
| **Total Official** | **42** | **7** | **21** | **5** | **15** | **7** |
| Independent | 13 | 2 | 0 | 0 | 0 | 1 |
| **Total** | **55** | **9** | **21** | **5** | **15** | **8** |

*Notes:* Media outlets included: ČTK, Telegraf, Hospodarska Noviny, Rudé Právo, Prague Radiožurnál, Mladá Fronta Dnes, Lidové Noviny, Ekonom, Pravo, Respekt, Denní Telegraf.
One 1995/96 piece was counted as two entries.

**SLOVAKIA**

| | Official Source | | Transcription | | Interview | |
|---|---|---|---|---|---|---|
| | 1993 | 1995/96 | 1993 | 1995/96 | 1993 | 1995/96 |
| Prime Minister | 1 | 0 | 1 | 2 | 0 | 2 |
| President | 1 | 0 | 1 | 1 | 0 | 0 |
| Foreign Minister | 5 | 0 | 2 | 1 | 1 | 0 |
| Defence Minister | 0 | 0 | 4 | 0 | 0 | 3 |
| Economics Minister | 0 | 0 | 0 | 1 | 0 | 0 |
| Finance Minister | 2 | 0 | 0 | 0 | 1 | 0 |
| Other Official | 12 | 8 | 7 | 0 | 1 | 1 |
| **Total Official** | **21** | **8** | **15** | **5** | **3** | **6** |
| Independent | 3 | 2 | 1 | 7 | 0 | 1 |
| **Total** | **24** | **10** | **16** | **12** | **3** | **7** |

*Note:* Media outlets included: Pravda, Rozhlasova Stanica, Bratislava TV, Bratislava Republika, Slovensky Dennik, Narodna Obroda, Smena, Sme, Slovenska Republika, Rozhlasova Stanica Slovensko Network.

minister, (2) the Cabinet challenging the president over NATO and the Council of Europe, (3) the chairman of the Christian Democratic Party (discussing a dispute between the prime minister and president), (4) the Green Party chairman's criticism of the environment ministry, (5) an independent US consultant criticizing the government's wage policy, (6) an economic institute in Vienna, and (7) the Civic Democratic Alliance.

Of the 21 articles reviewed in 1995–96, 19 used official sources in some capacity (seven as sources, five in transcription, and seven in interviews), and three relied on some sort of independent source as defined here. (One article had two sources, so was counted twice.) Of the 'other official' sources two were the mayor of a village challenging an agreement to change the Czech–Slovak border, and one was a military officer who 'wishe[d] to remain anonymous', discussing the dangers in Bosnia. The three 'independent' sources included an interview with the secretary of the Romany Democratic Congress, an industrial executive, and a report by an employers' association. While each of these three sources is here noted as independent, they each maintain highly visible leadership positions in the political and economic life of society.

*Slovakia*

Out of 43 articles reviewed in 1993, 39 relied on official sources (including 15 transcriptions and 3 interviews), and four on independent sources. The independent sources cited included a party chairman, a tank (weapons) plant manager (in an interview), and a group of tour bus drivers. The bus driver case is important because it is the only instance found here that uses explicitly unofficial sources. There are certain idiosyncracies about the official sources used, also. One of the foreign minister's citations was from a piece in which the minister was challenging certain tenets of *domestic* policy. Another piece described an International Monetary Fund official, an 'official source', criticizing Slovak economic policy. A third piece transcribed some of the Hungarian parliamentary deputies' complaints about the official visit of Romanian President Iliescu. The tendency to use official sources, especially as a way of raising a challenge or conflict 'objectively', and the deference to officialdom are all reflected in these cases. Finally, one piece on economic policy was based on a Central Bank report that was admittedly 'leaked' to the media. This reflects the mutual dependence of journalists and member of the government, as identified by Bethell.[5]

The 29 pieces from 1995–96 contained 19 that relied on official sources to some degree (including five transcriptions and six interviews). Of those, at least four were derived from journalistic contacts with individuals who provided their information anonymously. Of the ten articles citing independent sources five were derived from political party documents or statements. This is a questionable denotation of 'independent source', since in a parliamentary system political parties play a dominant role in organizing politics and government. Of the five other pieces with independent sources one included a trade union leader, another was an article written by an affiliate of the Economics University, and two were public opinion polls.

Two important trends are evident in this brief survey of media output in Eastern Europe. First, the use of official sources appears to be rather extensive. Further, the use of unnamed sources appears to be on the increase. The tendency for journalists to establish regular 'inside' contacts with officials, and to sustain their capacity to get information from these contacts by nurturing a deferential, uncritical relationship with the source, is common in Western press systems.[6] Unfortunately, such a relationship ultimately compromises the independent capacity of the journalist, as well as reflecting a decrease in journalistic initiative, two trends that do not contribute to higher-quality journalistic output.

Second, parliamentary parties are prominent sources of information, especially in the 1995–96 data. The increasing political capacity of parties may bode well for democracy, but their importance in the parliamentary system also makes them more akin to elite, if not 'official', sources. Furthermore, each party has its own level of commitment to internal democratic procedure, and so may only imperfectly reflect the interests of the population it claims to represent.

In either case, it appears that the news media are doing a good job of reporting official actions, statements and preferences, and doing a less adequate job of reporting independently acquired or gathered material.

*Explanatory Elements*

Following the content analysis approach employed by Graber,[7] a sample of pieces was drawn from the news media of Poland and Bulgaria (chosen for differences that exist similar to those between the Czech Republic and Slovakia), and the rate of coverage for the elements Who, What, Where, When, Why and How was measured. The pieces are all full text reprints in FBIS from January and February of 1994 and part of December 1995–January 1996.

The explanations of Why and How are here deemed particularly important aspects of reportage for two reasons: they help establish context, and they illuminate plausible causation. Here we should recall the distinction between the freedom of expression, which is protected by the right to publish, and the citizenry's access to information. Good information – appropriate context and useful explanation – is a necessary element of the social and political interaction that constitutes the reconstruction and maintenance of democratic society and institutions. Good explanation of the short-run economic consequences of the post-communist transition plays a particularly important role in the nurturing of political and economic liberalism. An introductory comparative politics text explains this phenomenon quite explicitly:

As these [post-communist Eastern European] societies move towards market economies, unemployment and prices will escalate, at least in the short and medium term. Populations with expectations of instant affluence for all will discover how costly is the transition to a market economy ... These countries may prove vulnerable to simplistic nationalist appeals from populist leaders offering instant solutions.[8]

learly, the observance of nationalist and populist political appeals does verify the failure of the press, but rather illustrates the importance of accurate and realistic economic and political information.

A few examples from the East European media illustrate this issue. In one of the pieces counted, the Polish authorities asserted that the *Washington Post* tried to make Poland (or the Polish government) look bad in the eyes of the Russians by claiming that Poland had sold Soviet weapons to the Americans in the early 1980s. The piece did not explain why or how (or, indeed, whether) this accusation would dishonour the current Polish government or Poland, nor did it elaborate the implications of the accusation for relationships among the three countries.

Another piece on Poland discussed the foreign minister's assertion that good relations with the East are important. Certainly nobody would question the importance of Poland's relations with any of its neighbours, but many would no doubt disagree over the relative importance or ordering of relations in specific issue areas. Neither the minister nor the media article discussed these aspects of the relations, or the connection between preferred outcomes and policy choices. A third piece discussed economic policy in Bulgaria: specifically, *why* the country needed an Export–Import Bank loan (to stabilize the economy) was mentioned, but *how* Export–Import loans stabilize economies (that is, how loan money is used) was not explained.

These omissions are important for at least two reasons. First, there is an inverse relationship between, on the one hand, assent over and consent to general unspecified policy ('good relations' instead of the specific kinds of good relations) and, on the other hand, democratic or pluralistic control over decisions. A greater range of decision for policy makers comes from reduced control by others, be they other officials or the public will. Obviously, the political system strikes a balance, which varies by issue, between flexibility and completely pluralistic decision-making, but the awareness of the trade-off involved in this inverse relationship is the point here. Second, specific to the East European countries and their economies, explanation and understanding of the context and causation in economic policy are vital to the prospect for both market and democratic reform. It is essential that the population should understand why and how the economy was ruined and how (and with what difficulty) it can be improved. It is with this understanding of the relevance of the news media's work that we should examine the informational content.

TABLE 2

EXPLANATORY ELEMENTS: BULGARIA AND POLAND

|  | Bulgaria | | Poland | |
|---|---|---|---|---|
|  | 1994 | 1995/96 | 1994 | 1995/96 |
| **Items counted** | **21** | **10** | **24** | **11** |
| Who | 21 | 10 | 24 | 11 |
| What | 20 | 10 | 24 | 11 |
| Where | 15 | 7 | 14 | 6 |
| When | 19 | 7 | 19 | 9 |
| Why | 7 | 5 | 8 | 6 |
| How | 3 | 2 | 5 | 2 |

*Notes:* Media outlets included the following:
   *for Bulgaria:* BTA, Khorizont Radio Network, Standart News, Bulgaria Armiya, Kontinent, Duma, Demokratsiya, 168 Chassa;
   *for Poland:* PAP, Warsaw TVP, Warsaw TVP Second Program, Polska Zbrojna, Rzeczpospolita, Radio Warszawa Network, Życie Warszawy, Gazeta Wyborcza, Radio First Program, Warsaw Trybuna, Poznań Wprost.

The pattern reflected in the results shown in Table 2 indicates the trends observed by Graber in American (TV) news. In both sets of media (American and Eastern European) the elements of Why and How are essential for a fuller understanding of issues, events and policy. In both cases these elements appear to go relatively less widely reported.

The patterns observed in the data for Poland and Bulgaria, and those for the Czech Republic and Slovakia, do not show a different result for a variation in the level of development of economic and civil society. Poland and the Czech Republic exhibit greater development of their respective economies or civil societies (or both) than do Bulgaria and Slovakia, but equivalent patterns of media performance are observed in all four countries. The second question this article addresses is why these patterns might exist. Specifically, why, when the news media of the Eastern European societies should be granted the opportunity to reconstruct themselves as independent organizations, have not they been so reconstructed?

## Institutional Analysis[9]

In his introductory essay O'Neil demonstrated that the literature on democratic transitions offers little insight either into the normative expectations of news media behaviour or into explanations of actual interaction between politics and the media. Institutional analysis, on the other hand, offers an understanding of political behaviour and results that may help. Specifically, the process of institutionalization yields an organizational arrangement that makes the establishment of a freer press system in the new East European democracies more difficult.

For the purposes of the present analysis we need to focus on the aspect of institutional approaches that sees institutionalization as, in the words of an early institutionalist, the '[infusing of the organization] with value beyond the technical requirements of the task at hand'.[10] In terms of Eastern Europe we shall see that the media as an institution of democratic politics have in fact become an indispensable tool for politicians, infused with the expectations of political support for the preferences of the ruling party.

The press in the communist period was an organ of the state, completely reliant on and subservient to the communist party. The argument advanced here is that the 'institutionalization of roles into statuses, of power into authority, and of precedent into norms reduces the role of the calculated exchange and introduces instead accommodations to the structure as it exists'[11] or, in this case, existed previously. In other words, radical change of the media's role and function is unlikely because the existing political organizational structure has not been sufficiently transformed. Specifically, the governmental structure, for example, a ministry of culture that oversees radio and television, including news, still exists, as it did in the communist period. This device gives ruling party politicians the opportunity to sustain an expectation of political support from the news media. These two circumstances reduce the independent ability of the news media to undertake efforts to improve their own performance (that is, to assert their political independence). The result is the persistence of an institution that performs sub-optimally.

We have seen that preliminary content analysis indicates that the East European news media exhibit a tendency to over-rely on official sources and to under-report important explanatory elements. Now I assert that these both result from the institutional legacies left by incomplete legal reform. One important legacy – perhaps the most important – comprises the political expectations for support placed by political actors on the news media.

### Legal Reform

The changes in press and media law in Eastern Europe follow a two-phase pattern: first, simple deconstruction of the communist structure, and, second, contentious reconstruction of new media law and organization. Frank Kaplan's discussion of Czechoslovakia captures this difference most succinctly: 'The immediate concern by the new government', he writes, 'following the revolutionary changes of November, 1989, was to eliminate the most constraining aspects of the existing press law and to begin thinking about formulating a totally new media policy future.'[12]

The deconstruction of the communist institutions and, more importantly, ideological predispositions occurred rapidly following the removal of the old governments. The descriptive and explanatory evidence comes most clearly from Czechoslovakia and Hungary, two of the more politically open, reform-minded, and economically developed countries.

In Czechoslovakia in early 1990, freedom of expression became a reality before the promulgation of any officially sanctioned amendment to the law which gave the communist party ultimate authority over the dissemination of information. Changes in the registration requirements for periodicals produced a proliferation of new publications that were formally approved by the official abolition of censorship in March 1990. At the same time the National Federal Assembly allowed individual citizens, including foreigners, to own and publish periodicals. In clarifying the new press freedom the new amendment to the press law also stated that 'In accordance with the institutionally guaranteed freedom of expression, word and press, citizens use the periodic press and other mass information media so that, through their facilities, they may obtain information and publicly express their views.'[13]

The distinction between obtaining information and expressing views is an important one. The organizing principle of the present study is the measure of the utility of the information to which the citizens of the East European countries now have access by means of their free presses.

In Czechoslovakia, the two-partner federation, now relieved of the political imposition of the Soviet system, had no mechanism for breaking the deadlock that arose over formulation of the new constitution. As a result, the 1960 Constitution remained in force while political negotiations continued. As Katarina Mathernova pointed out, the time available for such negotiation is impossible to estimate, though probably limited, because a fast-changing world will leave dawdlers behind.[14] While these specific negotiations led to the separation of the constituent Czech and Slovak nations, another crucial consequence is that the political interregnum left the institutions of the former regime in place, embedding themselves in the structure of the new regime.

The outcome in Hungary was quite similar to that of Czechoslovakia. In this case, a 1989 law changed the registration requirements, allowing anyone, including foreigners, to form a publication or publishing company, but the pluralism had actually originated a few years earlier. In May 1988, the long-time party secretary and prime minister, János Kádár, was replaced by Károly Grósz, and at the same time Imre Pozsgay assumed the position of minister of state. As a result of factionalism derived from their personal conflicts, Grósz began to used one of the official dailies, *Népszabadság*, to assert his positions, while Pozsgay used *Magyar Nemzet*. When Grósz relinquished the post of prime minister to Miklós Németh, Németh employed *Magyar Hírlap* to further his views. The political space created by the open factionalism within the party encouraged more of the formerly *samizdat* publications to speak out publicly. This slippery slope heading to expanding press freedom arrived at the reburial in June 1989 of Imre Nagy, the national hero of the 1956 revolution and icon of anti-Stalinism, for which all four national morning dailies offered expanded coverage. Such coverage of an event which the officials had difficulty reconciling with the party ideology spelled the end of the party's control of the press.[15]

The impact of these rapid changes on institutional reconstruction is uncertain, because the reconstruction has proceeded, in many ways, on an *ad hoc* basis. In Hungary for instance, a declaration by *Magyar Nemzet* on 3 July 1990 captures this, saying, 'There is no appropriate legal regulation for privatization [of the press], and there is no well-thought-out conception of how privatization should proceed.'[16] The essential problem consists in the political fact that the East European systems have been unable or unwilling to reconstruct the institution of the free press comprehensively.

Péter Paczolay asserts quite explicitly that the nature of the transition in Hungary has forced constitutional adjustment to the existing institutions, rather than the other way around. The nature, definition and organization of these institutions was based on the transitional deal arranged in 1989 by the communist party and the growing reform groups. Paczolay's point is that these political groups negotiated the transitional constitution, even though they possessed dubious legitimacy, especially in post-transition hindsight. Yet, the first freely elected parliament began to pass revisions and amendments to the transitional constitution, thereby enriching and legitimizing it. Decisions and interpretations of the constitutional court also contributed to this process – which eroded the political capacity to construct a wholly new constitution. Any effort to restructure the state's institutions or redefine rights would create a new discontinuity in the political and legal system.[17] Such a process may be inevitable, though. As the organizing and unifying principle of reform (opposition to the regime) recedes, the positive work of constructing a substantially new regime becomes too contentious. Marginal changes become more tolerable to the new variety of different political interests that had formerly united, primarily, in their opposition to the communist system.

The foregoing discussion makes it clear that the construction of institutions from whole cloth is politically unfeasible, so some institutional continuity will transcend the regime change. With respect to the press, the effect was more that the terms of the deconstruction of the old institution facilitated a rather hasty and *ad hoc* reconstruction, such as may not necessarily create the desired outcome. Karol Jakubowicz exposes this very problem in an article on rights of expression in post-communist East European constitutional reform, asserting that the first laws passed regarding the end of censorship 'arose from the first impatient impulse to create a new system primarily by negating the old one'.[18] Furthermore, many of the early laws on media reform sought to mix new openness with state control, or to depoliticize the state media, while leaving control in the hands of the state. The continuing state control of television and radio highlights this fact. Another problem revolves around ownership and privatization.

One element of this problem involves governments' inability to establish plans to privatize, primarily, electronic media in a way that facilitates the distribution of information. For instance, it took Hungary seven years to come up with a highly contentious plan to privatize some television services. Critics of the plan say that it really offers too little time and opportunity for the private holders of the television licence to establish their capacity to offer independent TV and information services. Körösényi may have indirectly shown the explanation for the difficulty in reaching even this contentious conclusion. He asserts that after having lost some of their dominance as leaders of the anti-communist coalition following the demise of the regime, intellectuals in Hungary seized on the media as a means of communicating their message.[19] The government became the target of intellectuals' attacks, which were undertaken through the media. In such circumstances the members of the government have less incentive to make such exploitation of the media even easier. Similar processes have certainly occurred in many of the other countries of Eastern Europe.

Western capital and experience are not necessarily the answer either, because they often come with a price. There is, no doubt, a gap between a foreign media company's ability to produce media services and the native raw, inexperienced enthusiasm for doing so. In Hungary, the new ability of foreigners to own publications seriously altered that country's media environment. The Western media entrepreneurs have a distinct advantage of skill and capital, so we should expect foreign capital to make strong intrusions into the Hungarian market. But these Western investments can come with Western demands. In 1989, Robert Maxwell invested in 40 per cent of *Magyar Hírlap* (a government daily), and demanded – and received – a new contract, regarding editorial appointments, with the government.[20] Not only do Western investors often attach conditions to their investment, but the rush to attract Western capital often results, as the *Magyar Nemzet* editorial of July 1990 pointed out, in privatization without direction. The result, in Hungary at least, is that some of the media outlets originally acquired by Western firms have been either abandoned or re-acquired by the state, leaving their long-term viability uncertain. In either case the availability of good information suffers.

### Political Control and Expectations about the Press

In the United States many government leaders have the expectation that the media's responsibility to society will be operationalized as support for the official line, and some in the media are not unsympathetic to such expectations. Some reject this mutual affinity, and others try to appear to do so.

East European official and media attitudes about the media manifest the same sorts of patterns. The patterns of concern here are those in which politicians expect the news media to support them, and those in which the critical or unsupportive news media are censured. The latter applies to one Czechoslovak newspaper that rejected the mutual affinity. In May 1992, *Telegraf* published lists of journalists who were suspected of being state security corps agents during the communist period, even though such publication might have been illegal. The editor of the paper defended the publication by saying that its purpose was to inform the public. In Slovakia, at least one media commentator preferred this action (and more) for Slovakia because the problem was deemed to be much more serious there.[21]

Such independence seems to be the exception, not the rule, while the political expectation of journalistic obeisance seems to be the rule. Since its separation from the Czech Republic, Slovakia has been a particularly difficult place for the operation of the newly free media. On the first business day of the country's independence the new government dismissed the editor of the largest independent daily. This means, of course, that this particular newspaper is not, in fact, independent. Moreover, before he became prime minister Mečiar promised, should he win power, to ban any journalists who criticized him. Robert Bonte-Friedheim, of The International Press Institute, surmised that because of threats like this the 'self-censorship of the Communist era'[22] was likely to return. The deputy prime minister also has weighed in with a proposal that is counterproductive for media freedom: in late 1993 he said that he thought a government council on media that could give tax breaks for various media, ostensibly to sustain production of less market-successful material, would be a good idea.[23] The possibility of using this programme as a way to reward the media preferred by the government and punish those disliked is obvious. Not all in the Slovak media would mind this, though. *Republika*, a pro-Mečiar paper, expressed concern that the media had been undermining 'national identity', and expressed dismay that those groups who had lost the elections still had strength and support in the media.[24]

Hungary, one of the most economically and socially developed of the East European countries, has seen some of the most intense difficulties. In early 1993 Elemér Hankiss, the director of Hungarian TV, and Csaba

Gombár, the director of Hungarian Radio, resigned their posts after a feud with Prime Minister Antall. The problems started when Antall tried to subsume budgetary control of the two agencies into the prime minister's office. In the process the media directors received letters from Antall saying that they no longer had control of their agencies, and also from President Göncz saying that they did. They resigned in protest, though they probably would have been dismissed anyway.[25] According to President Göncz, the subsequent result was that now all electronic media were 'under government control' and 'the opposition is unable to speak to the people'.[26] The government in turn claimed that opposition voices appeared more frequently than before. An FBIS analysis of ten Híradó (TV news) programmes shows that the opposition did appear frequently, but in ways that appear to minimize the impact. For instance, opposition speakers or politicians were often shown challenging less significant matters, and the government officials were always given the last word.

Many of the other countries of Eastern Europe exhibit similar sorts of problems. In March 1994, President Lech Walesa fired the chairman of the National Broadcasting Council in Poland, though he had 'no explicit legal right' to do so.[27] The deputy head of the presidential office claimed, however, that the president's right of dismissal was an implied power.[28] The fact that Walesa's decision was not challenged, and that the chairman of the Council accepted the firing, strengthens this 'implied' power. In Romania, legislation imposes a five-year prison term on anyone who commits 'public defamation of Romania and the Romanian nation', or gives 'false information and news posing a threat to state security and Romanian international relations'.[29] Romanian opposition figures fear this is a device to use against any who challenge the government. In Croatia, President Franjo Tudjman, who has questioned the loyalty of those who dissent from the official line, was reportedly trying to use the Fund for Development (the privatization agency) to buy print media, which would give the government control over both print and electronic media.[30] In Albania, an editor critical of the government was arrested as a security risk. He was asserted to have abetted the aggressive policies of the Yugoslav government.[31]

This list could go on, but two important trends stand out. First, not everyone in the government or the media has a resoundingly sanguine attitude about the role of the independent press. Second, the capacity (whether assumed or legally ascribed) for the government actually to *control* any part of the media will probably constrict media independence or opposition access, or both. State control (whether by ownership or by ministerial regulation) of any part of the media is part of the problem, because it does not meet the standard of independence in any model of a free press. The difference between state control and independence is all too clear. In Hungary, 80 per cent of all newspapers and magazines are privately owned, while TV and radio are largely state-operated. As Robert Bonte-Friedheim points out, the government has little capacity to control any of those print outlets, but it has substantial control over TV and radio.[32] Such control over electronic media is what really matters, though, since the trends in the consumption of news media are increasingly towards television viewing.

## Conclusion

This article has attempted to demonstrate that the political and organizational structures of the communist period have remained too intact for there to be a radical reorientation (that is, a freeing) of the news media in Eastern Europe. Politicians' attitudes towards the media described here are not particularly surprising. The media are often targeted by political demagogues, especially in trying times, to which economically weak countries are especially prone. The reliance on official sources and the lack of breadth of information content are important to recognize (and change) because the fragile, new democracies need strong institutions, to which independent media are central. The American media's mutual embrace with the state has followed a long period of fitful antagonism and independence. Even today, independence lost in one area may be compensated by the expression of new independence in hitherto untrodden territory.

A long history of antagonism and struggles for independence, and also a constitutional guarantee of freedom and independence (however determined), is quite a different matter from Eastern Europe's brief history that reflects an uneven record of setbacks as well as gains and an uncertain specification of the free press as a democratic institution. The observations made here reflect a real plausibility that the 'free presses' currently developing in Eastern Europe are trammelled by political manoeuvring, less diverse than they *ought to* or *could* be, and less informative than they need to be. Specifically, this article has found that attitudinal and institutional legacies have contributed to the gap between the hopes for free media and the media that actually exist in Eastern Europe.

These data, and the observations made from them, do not indicate that the news media are not more open, more energetic, more democratic, more informative, and more 'political' than during the communist period. The point of this study has not been to make comparisons between the two systems, as, in many ways, they are incomparable. Rather, the aim here has been to assess expectations and limits, to assess the character of the free press the East Europeans are really getting, and perhaps illuminate possibilities and difficulties they might face in the effort to reform their news media.

## NOTES

1. Robert Dahl, *Polyarchy* (New Haven, CT: Yale University Press, 1971).
2. Denis McQuail, *Mass Communication Theory: An Introduction* (Beverly Hills, CA: Sage, 1983); Fred Siebert et al., *Four Theories of the Press* (Urbana, IL: University of Illinois Press, 1956).
3. Leon Sigal, *Reporters and Officials: The Organization and Politics of Newsmaking* (Lexington, MA: Heath, 1973), pp.119–30.
4. Tony Atwater and Fred Fico, 'Source Reliance and Use in Reporting State Government: A Study of Print and Broadcast Practices', *Newspaper Research Journal*, No.8 (Fall 1986), pp.53–61, cited in James Lemert, *Criticizing the Media: Empirical Approaches* (Newbury Park, CA: Sage, 1989), pp.101–2.
5. Tom Bethell, 'The Myth of an Adversary Press', *Harper's*, Jan. 1977, pp.33–40.
6. Ibid.
7. W. Howard Public Lecture in Journalism and Mass Communication Research, Bloomington, IN, published by the Roy W. Howard Chair, School of Journalism, Indiana University, 1992.
8. Rod Hague, Martin Harrop and Shaun Breslin, *Political Science: A Comparative Introduction* (New York: St. Martin's, 1992), pp.123–4.
9. I am grateful to Patrick O'Neil for pointing me towards this literature. For a more thorough discussion of the organizational literature see his *Revolution from Within: The Hungarian Socialist Workers' Party 'Reform Circles' and the Transition from Socialism*, forthcoming, especially Ch.2.
10. Philip Selznick, *Leadership in Administration* (Evanston, IL: Row, Peterson, 1957), p.17, quoted in O'Neil, *Revolution from Within*, p.32.
11. Robert Bierstedt, 'Review of *Exchange and Power in Social Life*', *American Sociological Review*, Vol.30 (1965), p.790, quoted in Craig Calhoun and W. Richard Scott, 'Introduction', in Craig Calhoun, Marshall W. Meyer, and W. Richard Scott (eds.), *Structures of Power and Constraint: Papers in Honour of Peter M. Blau* (Cambridge: Cambridge University Press, 1990), p.10.
12. Frank Kaplan, 'Czechoslovakia's Press Law', in Al Hester and L. Earle Reybold (eds.), *Revolutions for Freedom: The Mass Media in Eastern and Central Europe* (Athens, GA: The James M. Cox, Jr. Center for International Mass Communication Training and Research, 1991), p.47.
13. Kaplan, 'Czechoslovakia's Press Law', p.47.
14. Katarina Mathernova, 'Czecho?Slovakia: Constitutional Disappointments', in A.E. Dick Howard (ed.), *Constitution Making in Eastern Europe* (Washington, DC: The Woodrow Wilson Center Press, 1993), pp.72–3.
15. Johnston M. Mitchell, 'The Evolution of a Free Press in Hungary, 1986–1990', in Hester and Reybold, *Revolutions for Freedom*, pp.139–46.
16. Ibid., p.154.
17. Péter Paczolay, 'The New Hungarian Constitutional State: Challenges and Perspectives', in Howard (ed.), *Constitution Making in Eastern Europe*, pp.30–31.
18. Karol Jakubowicz, 'Freedom vs. Equality', *East European Constitutional Review*, Summer 1993, p.43.
19. András Körösényi, 'Intellectuals and Democracy in Eastern Europe', *The Political Quarterly*, Vol. 65 (1994), pp.415–24.
20. Mitchell, 'The Evolution of a Free Press in Hungary', pp.148–50.
21. 'Publishing FIS List of Journalists Seen Possible', *Foreign Broadcast Information Service (FBIS)*, 30 April 1992, p.8; 'Names of Journalists Listed as StB Agents', *FBIS*, 5 May 1992, p.11; 'Editor Justifies Publication', *FBIS*, 5 May 1992, p.12; 'Slovak Media Seen under StB, Meciar Control', *FBIS*, 4 May 1992, p.14.
22. Robert Bonte-Friedheim, 'Nationalist Government Wages Brutal War on Media', *IPI Report*, Feb. 1993, p.7.
23. 'Kovac: Government Considering a New Media Body', *FBIS*, 7 Dec. 1993, p.14.
24. 'Daily Says Media "Undermining" National Identity', *FBIS*, 13 Dec. 1993, p.24.
25. Elemér Hankiss and Csaba Gombár, 'Why TV and Radio Heads Stepped Down', *IPI Report*,

Feb. 1993, p.6.
26. 'Hungary: Pro-Government Bias Taints Television News', *FBIS*, 22 Dec. 1993, p.32.
27. 'Walesa Dismisses Broadcasting Chairman', *FBIS*, 2 March 1994, p.18.
28. *East European Constitutional Review*, Country Update, Spring 1994, p.16.
29. Ibid., p.18.
30. 'Tudjman Widens Media Control, but Independent Voice Remains', *FBIS*, 21 April 1993, p.25.
31. 'Albania: Government Reverts to Old Ways, Arrests Critic', *FBIS*, 7 April 1993, p.33.
32. Robert Bonte-Friedheim, 'Box of Hope for the Freedom Lovers', *IPI Report*, Aug. 1993, p.20.

# Politics versus the Media in Poland:
# A Game without Rules

## TOMASZ GOBAN-KLAS

In Poland, substantial injections of foreign capital and ownership prerogatives have transformed the mass media from 1989 onwards, with French, Italian, Swiss, Norwegian, German and other involvement. This has affected both the range and style of both the printed and the broadcasting media. A struggle over ownership and control continued, however, notably over the control of the airwaves, particularly television. Ambivalent attitudes have delayed regulatory legislation, and the professional ethic of journalists in all media still owes much to the nineteenth-century tradition. Professional associations have not effectively raised professional standards, and the public is perplexed at the use that is made of the media. As Poland's democratic system develops, owners of communications media face a number of dilemmas that need to be resolved.

The media systems in Eastern Europe have been both the victors and the victims of the end of Communist rule.

– from a speech by Jane Curry, November 1992.

### Free at Last or Fettered Again?

In 1992 the enthusiastic cover of *Newsweek* declared the media in Eastern Europe 'Free at Last'. But soon it became obvious that new forms of control over the media are developing – that of legal regulation and that of market control. In addition, old habits die hard, and politicians still try, sometimes successfully, to use the media as instruments of power. The general situation of the media *vis-à-vis* politics and the state in the region has been thoroughly analysed by Karol Jakubowicz in his article 'Media Within and Without the State: Press Freedom in Eastern Europe'.[1] However, as the saying goes, the devil is in the details. Thus, the present article, focusing on Poland, adopts a different approach, centring on forces specific to the Polish case: in particular, on the role of the Roman Catholic Church.

Tomasz Goban-Klas is a professor in the Department of Sociology of Culture and Communication of the Jagiellonian University, Cracow, Poland.

## The New Media Landscape

After the political transition in August 1989, the Polish media began to undergo profound structural transformations that affected their legal and economic status. The groundwork for the transformation of the Polish media was initiated in mid-1989 when the procedure of licensing newspapers and magazines was replaced by a simple system of registration. Immediately, the press market began to flourish, in the number and quality of titles, if not in their circulation. Now, at least superficially, it resembles a press market in a Western country such as Italy. Publications are well printed, dailies with a good layout, weeklies in *Newsweek*-style format, women's weeklies and monthlies, computer, soft- and hard-core pornographic magazines, and hobby-related magazines for all special interests and tastes. However, this market is still unstable, dominated by foreign owners, with a strong element of continuity from the communist and pre-communist past.

Before the late 1980s, media ownership and control throughout Eastern Europe was rather simple. Radio and television were state-owned, while the print media were usually owned by political organizations, mostly by the communist party. Youth newspapers and magazines were owned by youth organizations, affiliated to the communist party. The control of the media was exercised directly by the communist party itself, and by state censorship, which in turn was controlled by the party,

After 1989, the media in Eastern Europe were transformed into self-managing commercial enterprises, which were at least technically independent. However, instead of ownership passing into the hands of national private owners such as journalists, investors or social organizations, these properties have been increasingly transferred into the hands of international media conglomerates.

The exact picture and scale of the foreign investment in the Polish media is not easy to portray (the same can be said of the other Central–East European countries). Most of the relevant data are not accessible, and, moreover, the situation is in constant flux; everything in this area remains dynamic.

## Major Polish Newspapers and Their New Owners

Before May 1989 in Poland there were 15 dailies with nation-wide distribution. Three years later, 19 national dailies were in print. Of this number, ten targeted the public at large, three were sports dailies, two rural papers, two financial dailies, one directed toward children, and one for the military.

The new daily, *Gazeta Wyborcza*, now the most widely read daily in Poland, was born in 1989 as the unofficial organ of Solidarity. The paper proudly carried Solidarity's logo and a masthead that proclaimed 'There Is No Freedom Without Solidarity'. From its inception, *Gazeta Wyborcza* was owned by Agora, a limited liability company established in April 1989 by the famous film director, Andrzej Wajda, and two Solidarity leaders, Aleksander Paszynski and Zbigniew Bujak; Lech Walesa nominated the well-known dissident Adam Michnik to be editor-in-chief. The company grew quickly, using the old press equipment that the French daily *Le Monde* had donated when it modernized its facilities. *Gazeta* is primarily Polish-owned, although at least ten per cent of its shares have been sold to an American media company, Cox Communications. It also publishes the weekly section *Wall Street Journal/Eastern Europe*.

After *Gazeta*, *Rzeczpospolita* is the second most important Polish national daily, and the most serious. Formerly a government organ, after privatization *Rzeczpospolita* changed to a limited liability company as a joint venture of the Polish government and the French company Socpress (owned by the press baron Robert Hersant) and the paper itself. Foreign investments helped to make *Rzeczpospolita* an almost independent, information-based paper. However, in 1992, the government began to regret its decision to sell shares and attempted to regain editorial control over the daily, but by that time it was too late to make the daily a mouthpiece for the government once again. *Rzeczpospolita* still listens to the government, giving it a place to publish its views, but thanks to its financial independence does not necessarily support it.

Established in 1944, *Życie Warszawy* is the oldest of the existing dailies in Poland. In 1991, the paper became the property of a newly established company, Società Televisiana Italiana, several Polish companies, and Varsovia Press –whose shareholders consist of *Życie Warszawy*'s editor-in-chief and 45 staff journalists. In 1993, most of the Polish shares were sold to the Italian partner, whose total participation in the company rose to over 80 per cent.

A second Warsaw daily, *Express Wieczorny*, which was for many years the most widely read Warsaw evening paper, was initially purchased by the Solidarity Press Foundation to promote its cause and turn a profit. In 1993 it was bought by the Swiss media concern JMG Ost Presse Jorg Marquard. *Sztandar Mlodych*, a former communist youth daily, was published by the Economic Education Foundation, the Polish Culture Foundation and Polskie Nagrania, a record company. Later over 35 per cent of its shares were sold to an Austrian group, and subsequent to that it was sold again to Fibak-Marquard Press and JMG Ost Presse Jorg Marquard.

As is clear from the cases outlined above, the process of political and economic changes in Poland has created conditions whereby foreign investors have been able to buy into the Polish media system. At the beginning of this year (1996), the foreign investors owned some 56 per cent of the total share of Polish national dailies. These dailies in turn have 70 per cent of total national circulation. Foreign investors also control 50 per cent of Polish regional dailies, which in turn hold some 65 per cent of the total circulation in that segment.

Foreign capital has also been invested in Polish magazines, whose circulation tops 15 million copies a week. Currently on the Polish media market there are a number of so-called 'carbon copies' of Western magazines (especially those patterned after German youth publications) such as *Tina*, *Dziewczyna* (Girl), and *Popcorn*. There are also Western-style TV guides, Polish versions of *Playboy*, *Elle* and *Scientific American*. Other examples of substantial foreign investment include such financial publications as *Gazeta Bankowa*, owned primarily by the firm French Expansion, and *Business Week/Poland* by McGraw-Hill. The Norwegian conglomerate Media Orca has also been active in the Polish market. In general, the most active in the Polish press market are German media conglomerates, such as Neue Prassauer Presse, which recently bought out the shares owned by the French publishing firm Hersant, and Heinrich Bauer Verlag.

Another important source of investment is Italian. The financial daily *Nowa Europa* (New Europe) is controlled by Italian group Il Sole–24 Ore, of Milan. A second Italian group, Fininvest (owned by Berlusconi), also has been involved not only in buying shares in the daily *Życie Warszawy*, but also in setting up an illegal television network, Polonia 1, whose programming was based on old TV soap operas, mostly Brazilian in origin. When the network was refused a TV licence (allegedly promised by President Walesa's top advisers) by the state National Council for Radio and Television, Polonia 1 went on satellite and now it broadcasts from Rome. In the meantime, President Walesa, acting at the margin of his legal powers, replaced three members of the Council, and there are rumours that Polonia 1 might get its licence in the near future.

*Radio Fun*, now known as RMF (Radio, Muzyka, Fakty), began in 1989 in Cracow. The station was launched by the newly established Foundation for Social Communication, a brainchild of the round-table agreement, which called for more pluralism in the media. The foundation was supported financially by Polish émigrés in France with the political backing of a Polish senator, who had chaired the media talks at the round table and later became the minister for internal affairs. With such influential supporters, the station easily received a temporary permit to operate, although initially it could broadcast only in French. The programme was initially a satellite re-transmission of the Paris-based network Radio Fun. After a year, it was allowed to broadcast in Polish, and became a domestic outlet.

The Polish press over time has become more pluralistic but not truly independent. Most Poles continue to see the press as more political than objective. It has been widely believed that each party or faction must have a newspaper as its mouthpiece and that every newspaper must have some affiliation with a party or a faction. The main focus of concern for publishers and journalists has been the economic obstacles that at present constitute a barrier to a free and independent press. Printing and newsprint are extremely expensive, their costs skyrocketing after the economic reform programme was introduced in 1990. Large city newspapers rely on advertising for a surprisingly high percentage of their revenue. *Życie Warszawy* draws 70 per cent of its revenue from advertisements, and *Gazeta Wyborcza* receives about 60 per cent.

### Readers' Likes and Dislikes

In the early 1990s, there was an increase in the circulation and sales of the following types of magazines:

- so-called light papers, especially magazines providing sensational criminal stories (*Detektyw, Skandale, Sensacje, Kobra*); those with mixed content (sensationalism, politics and sex), such as *Raport*; and erotic magazines (in particular *Cats*, the Polish edition of *Playboy*);

- shoppers' and advertising magazines (such as *Top, Kontakt* and many other local free papers);

- pop music papers and fan magazines (such as *Magazyn Muzyczny, Rock 'n Roll* and others), and 'audiovisual' magazines that deal with the new media (*Audio-Video, TV-Sat Guide* and the Polish edition of *PC World*);

- horoscopes and 'semi-scientific' papers, as *Nie z tej ziemi* (Incredible), *Nieznany Świat* (Unknown World), *Szaman* and *Sfinks*);

- news magazines, such as *Wprost* (Direct).

The readership of certain types of magazines has remained largely stable; this is particularly the case with women's magazines, mainly because new, more attractive titles have appeared, such as *Twój Styl* (Your Style), youth periodicals and certain 'highbrow' magazines, such as *Nowa Res Publica* and *Puls*. In contrast, the free-market economy has not helped the Catholic press flourish. *Tygodnik Powszechny*, the most prestigious of Catholic papers, previously sold approximately 70,000 copies and at its height reached a circulation of 140,000; at present, and with much difficulty, it manages to sell barely 40,000.

By far the most spectacular emergence in the new press has been the blasphemous weekly run by Jerzy Urban, the former government spokesman under martial law. Urban launched the satirical weekly *Nie* (No) in October 1990; six months later he was selling a staggering half a million copies a week, mostly as a result of the paper's concentration on making fun of Poland's new rulers and the Roman Catholic church, ribald drawings and photos, and anything that smacked of scandal.[2] In 1980, the average circulation of all newspapers was slightly above ten million copies. In the following years, circulation fell slowly but steadily. According to 1990 estimates, total circulation had fallen to 5.1 million copies – almost half of what it had been at the beginning of the decade. In 1991, there was an increase in the total circulation of newspapers to 5.3 million copies.

### The Long Battle over the Airwaves

Since the end of the 1980s the debates on the media have been most intensively concentrated in the area of television. In June 1991, the Sejm decided that until the new broadcasting law was adopted there would be a moratorium on broadcasting frequencies. When the law did not materialize, in February 1992 a group of parliamentarians demanded an amendment to the bill on telecommunications that would allow for the temporary allotment of frequencies to some of the more than 800 interests that had petitioned for licences.

The lack of a new media law was wholly connected with political struggles inside parliament. In the fall of 1991, parliament considered two competing broadcasting bills. One, introduced by the Peasant Party, was in response to complaints that the state-owned broadcasting services favoured the government and denied the party adequate access to their facilities. The bill provided for direct parliamentary supervision of the country's broadcasting service. The second was a government bill, and provided for the establishment of a national broadcasting council to assign frequencies, grant licences and handle all regulatory functions.[3] Its 11 members would be chosen by parliament and the government; state-owned radio and television services would then become a public service corporation. In addition, private citizens would have the right to own broadcasting stations on the FM band. The downside to this part of the proposal was that new transmitters and new types of radios would be required if the higher spectrum of the FM band were to be employed in Poland.

However, the bill was not approved by the Senate, because most parliamentarians were not satisfied with one statement within the proposal: 'Programmes may not propagate actions, attitudes and opinions contradicting public morals.' Several senators demanded the replacement of the weak word 'morals' with the much stronger term 'Christian ethics'.[4]

Other areas of debate also took a great deal of time and energy. One lengthy discussion concerned foreign investments. In all proposed bills regulating broadcasting, foreign ownership was restricted to a range between 20 per cent (which was considered insufficient for the modernization of broadcasting) and 33 to 40 per cent. In an attempt to salvage at least part of its efforts, parliament hastily prepared a new, abbreviated and limited bill. It was referred to as the 'little bill', because it dealt only with the setting up of private commercial stations. In late 1991, this was passed by the slimmest of parliamentary majorities.[5] Immediately, the new law was widely criticized as being too narrow and flawed. The president was, therefore, advised not to sign it, and he did not.

In 1992, the government finally prepared a second bill that simply repeated the provisions of the 1960 charter regarding government control over state broadcasting.[6] Three years after the start of the media debate, parliament approved the new radio and television law in late December 1992. Like its predecessor, it too was far from perfect, particularly with regard to its establishment of a form of censorship. The law stipulates that radio and television, both public and private, have to 'respect the Christian system of values as a basis, while accepting universal ethical principles [and] the Polish state's vital interests'. The law does not explain what these requirements entail. For the spokesman for Christian–National Alliance (ZChN), the main party supporting this legislation, 'the Christian values are simply there'. But no one is clear on specifics. According to a survey of clergy and politicians, for instance, some consider that teaching young people about the use of condoms would be in line with a Christian system of values, while many others do not agree.

The law also instituted a National Council of Radio and Television (KRRiT), responsible for the allocation and supervision of the airwaves. The council consists of four persons appointed by the Sejm, two by the Senate, and four by the president. Their appointments are to last up to four years, but the council may be dissolved if parliament and the president fail to approve its annual report. Instead of being an arm of the state, the council is essentially dependent upon the current political situation. It has also become in effect a censoring agency, jokingly referred to as the National Council of Airwaves Inquisition, because it has the duty to grant or revoke licences on the basis of a vague concept of 'Christianity'.

A foretaste of this was seen in the controversy created by a song and a poster. In this case, ZChN induced the district attorney to prosecute the rock group Piersi (Breasts) for performing a song entitled 'ZChN's Coming', which is sung to the tune of the hymn 'Jesus Christ Is Coming'. The words describe a priest visiting one of his parishioners. During his visit, the priest consumes a great quantity of vodka, speeds off in his luxury Toyota, and crashes into a fence. The parishioners complain that they will have to put more money into the collection plate. Officially, ZChN explained the suit by stressing the song's offensive view of religion. A producer at the state radio station was eventually fired, apparently for giving the song airplay, and, although he was later reinstated through the intervention of some parliamentary deputies, the song was no longer played on public radio. Despite this, the song instantly became a hit on the cassette market, and when Piersi performed it publicly, some 9,000 young people sang along with the band.

In another case, a huge poster advertising Benetton, the well-known Italian clothing company, portrayed a priest kissing a nun. The local authorities in many cities, including the capital, Warsaw, immediately banned the advertisement. ZChN also called for a ban on sales of the Polish translation of Salman Rushdie's *Satanic Verses*. Later, ZChN's leader accused a television cabaret programme of being especially dedicated to ridiculing Catholics, which was in his opinion a criminal act. Demanding the banning of the programme, he added that 'Poland is a country of religious tolerance, because in Muslim countries the producer would have had her throat slit long ago for such acts of blasphemy'. By early 1993, circumstances had developed to such a point that one columnist from a fundamentalist Catholic weekly openly called for 'setting up sane, humane, and patriotic censorship'.[7] This was too much, even for many Catholics. Józefa Hennelowa, a commentator from the moderate Catholic weekly *Tygodnik Powszechny*, wrote an open letter to the chairperson of the Association of Catholic Journalists protesting against this appeal, but the reply publicly sustained the idea of amending the press law in a way that would defend 'ethical and humane values'.

In response, 29 eminent Polish writers and literary critics published an open letter defending freedom of speech. It was the first act of open, public defiance of the church's stand since the fall of communism. The letter was brief and forceful, declaring that 'as a person regarding highly the freedom of speech, I am against any legislation – that is, laws and decrees – which could form a basis for by-laws and rules introducing hidden or open censorship'.[8]

## Journalists at a Loss

Paradoxically, freedom of the press did not bring greater independence for journalists, at least for most of them. Theoretically, anyone can now set up his or her own daily or weekly, but for many reasons, especially because of distribution problems, this it is not a viable option. Journalists are now free. However, unemployment is a new and serious concern. In 1991 alone, more than 2,000 journalists lost their jobs for economic reasons.[9] A smaller number were fired or received early pensions for political reasons. This process continued well into the following year. One example is that of Jacek Snopkiewicz, a veteran journalist who was fired several times by the communist media. After the victory of Solidarity, he was nominated to be managing editor of an important and influential television evening bulletin. Yet, despite his efforts to be as independent as possible (or perhaps because of them), he was fired one year later by new television management.[10] Then, as editor-in-chief of the popular daily of the Democratic Party, *Kurier Polski*, he survived another year, only to be fired by party leadership with the explanation that they no longer 'shiver[ed] in fear when taking the paper in their hand'.[11] However, it is usually journalists who tremble and not publishers. The fear of losing a job pushes journalists to accept any working conditions and, perhaps worse, to follow orders from their managing editors.

The most serious obstacle to the independence of the Polish media is the lack of a professional code among journalists.[12] Most of those remaining from the days of communism want to relegitimize themselves; they lack the courage to challenge public ideas, whether those of the government, the church or a pop star. They are afraid to think critically, to probe or to question.[13] There are some notable exceptions, among the elite newspapers, such as *Rzeczpospolita* and *Życie Warszawy*.

Some, usually the youngest, newcomers to the profession represent the opposite extreme. Instead of tacitly accepting information from official sources, they criticize everyone and everything, using vulgar language and seeking out sensational stories at any cost. Having insufficient experience and knowledge of the topics on which they report, they usually blur the line between reporting and opinion. This is evident in some television public affairs programmes and in several sensationalist political dailies, such as *Super Express* or *Gazeta Polska*.

The most visible result of these problems is the low quality of journalists' editorial work in terms of their frequent factual mistakes, such as misquoting sources or omitting important data. Usually only one-sided stories are published – either for or against. Those journalists who had worked for the anti-communist opposition and who at present hold managerial and editorial positions in media publications have no experience in producing well-balanced perspectives and views. Negation of the system was the principle of their work, and that work was only a negative reflection of official statements: black was white and white was black. What was needed was the civic courage to articulate opposing views. The experience from the underground press thus translated into 'normal' press, in that publications were not to practise critical, independent, factual, objective journalism.

The present psychological stalemate can be explained by both historical and sociological factors, particularly the traditional role of the journalist in Poland and in Eastern Europe in general. As far back as nineteenth-century Poland, a journalist was a person who received some literary education but was not talented enough to become a writer of novels. Polish newspaper workers were never dedicated professionals who provided information, but were usually educators, politicians, propagandists and creative writers. Under communist rule, the journalist was a living 'transmission belt' between the party and society. Thus objectivity, professional values and professional ethics took different meanings from what they held in traditional, liberal journalism. Therefore, these legacies, both old and new, sustained the role of journalists as the teachers, preachers and spiritual leaders of society.

While journalist associations might be viewed as a potential solution to these problems, the role of such organizations in developing press freedom and professionalism has been very small. There are two major journalist organizations in Poland, each struggling with the other for a major share of the assets of the old communist-era journalists' union. The two organizations have so far been able only to issue an occasional lofty statement demanding further democratization of the media and formulation of a new government information policy. Little has been done to implement new principles, ethical codes and the like. Yet they should not be blamed entirely for this; their impotence reflects the low prestige of the profession among the political elite and the public at large.[14]

It is paradoxical that journalists, who actually had such an important impact on the dismantling of the system, have lost much of their influence on the public. In 1991, the media could not mobilize society to take part in the first free parliamentary election in Poland in 50 years, when turnout was only 40 per cent. Perhaps this was a result of the alienation of the media system from Polish society. The language and the views of the media still reflect the ideas and opinions of only one social stratum – the Polish intelligentsia. The media audience itself was the one category that in the past was treated as if it were the least important element in the communication system, and this legacy still influences journalistic actions. The mass media continue to be fundamentally deficient in terms of their comprehensiveness, objectivity and professionalism. This view is shared across the political spectrum, although the criticism stems from different perspectives and interests. Nevertheless, it is usually well documented. Even when the media try to separate news and opinion, they still continue to perform an advocate function. The most popular daily, *Gazeta Wyborcza*, cannot resist commenting on all important news reports with signed commentaries in bold font. The media are still far from truly autonomous and objective, and many politicians prefer that they serve as a political trumpet rather than an independent information agency. Nowhere can this be more clearly seen than in the debates on the broadcasting act.

## Enter the Roman Catholic Church

As an institution seeking to extend the freedom of religious practice and to promote Christian values, the church proved to be the clear winner in the confrontation between the old regime and Solidarity. It gained a dominant position within Polish television and, to a lesser extent, radio. Its position has been based formally on an official agreement between the communist government and the Episcopate made in May 1989, but it stems more from the moral and political power that the church acquired during its prolonged struggle with communism in Poland.

In fact, the church embodies the most ancient and exalted ideas of traditional Polish life.[15] It has long been a part of the world of Polish politics, culture, and society – sometimes in the forefront, always in the background. Fidelity to the church became synonymous with faithfulness to the spirit of the Polish nation.[16] The convergence of religion and national consciousness nursed both Catholicism and nationalism. Under communism, the church's direct mass media influence was limited to a few papers officially regarded as Roman Catholic (that is, those having a 'Church assistant' on the editorial board). Beginning in September 1980, these papers were supplemented by religious radio broadcasts, a gain won by the striking Gdansk workers.

Paradoxically, then, martial law increased the prestige and possibilities of the church in Poland. The ruling generals were more willing to allow the church to operate than they were to tolerate Solidarity; the church was the only legal oppositional institution, and remained so to the end of the decade. It equipped thousands of parish centres with video cassette recorders, organized video shows of underground political films, supported Catholic discussion clubs, and, most importantly, influenced editors and journalists of many papers to relay the church's position.

Since mid-1989, the church has had its own television programmes. The new Law on Telecommunication passed in 1991 gave priority to the Roman Catholic church when new radio frequencies are allocated. The reason given for this was that the church should be treated preferentially because it had the right (under a separate 1989 Law on State–Church relations) to have access to the airwaves.[17] As a result, the church now has a very visible presence on television, with such regular programmes as the *Evening Prayer*. In many other broadcasts, including news bulletins and talk shows, the clergy also frequently appear.

As be might expected, the church has not been satisfied with the

performance of lay journalists. In a communiqué of the Conference of the
Polish Episcopate on 21–22 June 1991, criticism of the media was quite
strong:

> The bishops also considered some damaging phenomena in the mass
> media. For some time, there has been disturbing content that clearly
> ridicules the truths of the faith and moral norms. They are also
> perceived by many faithful as blasphemous. These phenomena cannot
> be in agreement with an elementary culture of common living, with
> basic rights of humans, and with true tolerance. The faithful have
> rights, and the duty, to demand respect for their religious beliefs in all
> public communications.[18]

In September 1991, a thunderbolt struck. From all pulpits in the country
a pastoral letter was read that contained a harsh assessment of journalists,
accusing them of

> losing elementary sensitivity to the basic and the most important
> problems of the nation and the state. Instead, they expose marginal or
> secondary issues. They do not teach to a sufficient extent the love of
> the motherland. The writers do not understand the historical
> transformations in Poland. They do not undertake attempts to
> mobilize reliable and scrupulous work for the public good.[19]

The bishops considered the Polish media at the time as incapable of working
for social integration and the rebuilding of community bonds. They claimed
that without deep and broad reforms, 'the media would inevitably lead us to
divisions and quarrels'.[20]

Unfortunately, the church provided neither good nor bad examples;
therefore, it was not clear what was meant by writing in the communiqué
that 'the clear hope for the future is found in certain new periodicals and
certain radio and television programmes'. It was obvious, however, that
these did not include the respected Catholic *Tygodnik Powszechny*, whose
editor-in-chief had criticized the Episcopate's stand on the media.

Of course, the church has no formal power to control the contents of
programming, and its influence is rather weak in the general-interest press.
However, indirect church influence and control, especially in broadcast
media, are obvious to all participants in the media system. In this area the
church has prepared a communication doctrine for the national media,
which in a draft version argued that 'the church in Poland has to embrace,
by its pastoral care, those in the media. They are in need of spiritual support
in order to serve truth and human beings. This refers to all mass media, not
only to those under church patronage.'[21]

One of the main issues of concern for the Polish church has been the widespread use of obscenity in the printed media. Without censorship, it is possible only to control the media through the press law and those penal code provisions against pornography. The church's position apparently influenced the attorney general when, in the spring of 1991, he issued a memorandum suggesting the urgent need to prosecute editors who published pornography. The response was a court action against the editor-in-chief of the anti-establishment satirical weekly, *Nie*, on the charge of publishing a pornographic drawing. In July 1991, the district attorney of Warsaw summonsed the editor-in-chief Urban, asserting that many citizens complained that materials in the weekly were insulting to their religious feelings. He added that similar trials should be expected, because there were many other such publications. Despite pressures on the court from the attorney general's office, however, Urban was eventually acquitted: the judge did not consider the illustration to be truly pornographic.

In order to effect long-term changes in the current media context, the church also began to promote special schools and training for journalists in the Catholic press, radio, and television. Attempts to formalize church influence could be seen within the context of a new journalistic association, the Association of Catholic Journalists, especially in its statutory provision that members may simultaneously participate in other journalist associations. The biggest church gain within the media was, however, the new law on radio and television which was eventually enacted in 1993. This law contains a provision concerning 'respect for Christian values' by both public and private broadcasters. In addition, indirect church influence over the broadcast media could be seen in the process of licensing new radio and television networks. The Polish episcopate officially endorsed one of the petitioners out of ten applicants, and this person (it was in fact one citizen) was subsequently granted the privilege of operating the single national private television network for the next ten years. Although the same strategy did not work as well in the area of radio broadcast licensing, the church network Radio Maryja was permitted to operate on a national scale.

## Communications at the Crossroads

The opposition to communist control over the media has always stressed faith in an independent, vigorous, pluralistic media. It demanded limiting and eventually abolishing censorship, and creating a free marketplace of ideas; it constantly praised the concept of media independence and autonomy. When some of these conditions materialized and the media began to speak with their own voice, it also began to criticize those in power. Moreover, it began to cater to the needs of the less educated. Intellectuals and new political elites in turn desired media loyalty to themselves; they themselves soon began to complain about the media and to blame journalists for all social and political evils.

Instead of the expected pluralism within the framework of Solidarity political consensus, a new kind of media polyphony appeared, although to the ears of many new politicians it sounded more like a cacophony. This has not been a uniquely Polish phenomenon. All over Eastern Europe the media are being accused of irresponsibility and of being too 'liberal'. New governments and new political parties alike have not been satisfied with the media's performance. The media have many strong critics and only a few, rather weak, supporters.

The media debates in post-communist countries today are fierce and passionate, but the arguments are weak. There are no Eastern European Miltons or Mills to whom they can refer; nor is there a tradition of using European political philosophy as a basis for the defence of freedom of speech and of the press. Perhaps this is due to historical factors; Poles have traditionally been more concerned with the preservation of the nation, national culture and religion against foreign oppression than with individual civil and citizens' rights.[22] It should be noted that the liberal intelligentsia has returned to the policy of writing open letters – formerly used against the old regime to call for civil rights and freedom of expression – though now the targets are the non-communist government and the Roman Catholic church. The target may have changed, but the wording and arguments are very similar.[23]

The struggle for control over the media – on the part of media elites to sustain their editorial autonomy and on the part of ruling elites to sustain their power – is based on several false assumptions and some justified concerns. Both sides want to strengthen the democratic system. The conservative–nationalist political parties and the Roman Catholic church perceive themselves as an emanation of the national will and view their main task as preserving national culture and spirit. Both groups believe that the media wield enormous power over the people. They consider media to be not *a* major but *the* main instrument of politics. Their vision of the media is one-dimensional, over-politicized and simplified, believing in a missionary role for journalists and an idealized press. Ideological discourse in post-communist media policy debates is also marked by a deep feeling of insecurity among the media elites and the ruling political forces. Each is afraid of the other, and politicians fear their constituencies. They believe they are unfairly attacked and they respond with attacks of their own. It should be stressed, however, that this is not a typically Polish feature of the media controversy. The same underlying assumptions can be discerned in other Eastern European countries, particularly Hungary.[24]

### New Battles Between the Press and the Judiciary

Such tension has eventually crept into the area of legal prosecution. In December 1994, a reporter investigating police corruption in Poznan spent 12 hours in prison after being charged with deceiving a police officer. In January 1995 the Polish Supreme Court ruled that in certain conditions a prosecutor or a court can waive reporters' right to confidentiality. In April 1995, a Polish reporter, Marcin Mastalerz, was sentenced to six months in prison (suspended for two years) and 1,000 zloty in fines plus court costs for obstruction of police operations. By impersonating a French tourist victimized by a pickpocket, he tried to discover the fate of a foreigner in trouble. A spokesman for the Ministry of Justice said: 'It is important to realize that a journalist, like any other citizen, is not above law.'[25]

In January 1996, after three years of proceedings, the controversial owner and editor-in-chief of *Nie* weekly, Jerzy Urban, was given a two-year suspended prison sentence, fined, and banned from working as a journalist and editor-in-chief of any paper for disclosing in print a classified note that a prominent member of Walesa's staff had previously been an informer of the communist secret police.

### The New Journalism and Media

Polish political journalism created a new style which can be labelled 'rap' journalism, which means a style of writing and interviewing that begins with a definite political standpoint and an aggressive stance. The object of this rap journalism (which is quite visible in Polish public television) is primarily the ruling coalition, which is composed of ex-communist social-democrats and peasant parties. There is a strong cognitive dissonance between facts and opinions expressed by journalists and the majority of the voting public, which makes the media less credible and less politically influential. Almost all the mass media, including television, were clearly against the leftist presidential candidate, Aleksander Kwasniewski of the Democratic Left Alliance, in the 1995 election; yet, by not responding to the attacks in a similarly aggressive fashion, Kwasniewski was able to win the votes of the younger generation, and as a result, the election.

In summary, we can outline some distinctive features of the present-day media in Poland:

* the media system is dynamic, but also fragmented and contradictory;

* the past, both communist and pre-communist, influences the present, especially regarding thinking about the media – how its roles, power, functions and tasks are conceived by political elites, by the Roman

Catholic church, by journalists and by the public at large;

- publishers and, to a lesser extent, editors and journalists are engaged in reinventing the media system and are redefining their roles within the context of a market economy;

- the media scene is in a state of flux; there are constant changes in top positions. Each prime minister nominates his or her confidants to the government media. Journalists quarrel among themselves, sue one another, despise each other. In the meantime, political 'verification' ('lustration') has been in place since 1989;

- The quality of journalistic output is mixed, and there is growing discontentment with the results of journalists' work. Conservative politicians accuse the media of being a destructive force in society, mainly because of their social irresponsibility, lack of ethical basis and poor journalistic education: indeed, the light-hearted coverage of some alleged bank machinations caused financial losses and customer panic. Left-wing politicians, however, complain that the media are predominantly rightist and that they distribute biased information about the Left.

- The media mainly perform an advocacy role, still connected to government (electronic broadcasting) or political parties or factions (the press), rather than being truly independent.

**Some Predictions**

We must now ask what the future holds for the post-communist Polish media. What will their role be when old-style dissent and critical reports focusing on étatism and socialism no longer exist? What will be the new target or targets? Gender and women's issues, ecology, nationalism, anti-Semitism, or, perhaps, business and democracy? Will the quality press develop, or will it be replaced by sensationalist tabloids?

What will become of state broadcasting? Will it find a competitor in sound, private, commercial broadcasting, or be renamed as 'public' and continue as a semi-monopolistic organization?

These questions are now impossible to answer. Let me, rather, delineate some dilemmas facing media controllers, owners and personnel:

- Commercialization or politicization?

- Specialized or mass media?

- Privatization or monopolization of ownership?

- Deregulation or centralization of state control?

- Westernization or nationalization of content?
- Modernization or deterioration of the media facilities?
- Secularization or Christianization of media values?

In an analysis of the Italian public sphere, Paolo Mancini identified four fundamental characteristics that differentiate the media in Italy from those in a number of Western European democracies, particularly in the Anglo-Saxon countries:

(1) The media are under strong state control, either directly as in case of state-owned television or indirectly as in various cases of presses that are state-owned or economically supported, or both.

(2) The degree of mass media partisanship is strong: 'the political parties have always been involved in editorial choices and the structure of mass media'.

(3) Equally strong is the degree of integration of the media and political elites: for example, there is a strong professional mobility between the worlds of politics and journalism.

(4) There is no consolidated and shared professional ethic among media professionals.[26]

These four characteristics of the Italian system are surprisingly close to the present situation in East–Central Europe.

## NOTES

1. *Journal of Communication*, Vol.45, No.4 (Autumn 1995), pp.125–39.
2. 'We are in tune with social attitudes', the editor explained: quoted from an article concerning the Polish press: 'Free at Last', *Newsweek*, 10 June 1991, p.21.
3. 'The Bill of the Law on Radio and Television, 13 September 1991', *Przekazy i Opinie*, Nos.3–4 (1991), pp.62–73.
4. This stance was obviously influenced by church demands. The bishops asked rhetorically: 'Just who are parliamentary deputies representing when, in a country with a decisive majority of Christians, they reject a motion to respect the Christian value system in the mass media?': see *Slowo Powszechne*, 19 Oct. 1992, p.1.
5. The Law on Broadcasting, 19 Oct. 1991, unpublished.
6. The same stalemate occurred in Hungary, Czechoslovakia and Romania.
7. Danuta Mastalska, 'Polska wieza Babel', *Niedziela*, 21 Jan. 1993, p.7.
8. *Gazeta Wyborcza*, 29 Jan. 1993, p.1.
9. According to estimates by the Association of Journalists of the Republic of Poland.
10. Snopkiewicz published a book about his editorship, a very revealing depiction of the internal pressures in post-communist television: *Dziennik Telewizyjny* (Warsaw: BWG, 1991).
11. *Gazeta Wyborcza*, 12 Feb. 1992, p.2.
12. In theory, the Polish journalists' code of ethics is among the oldest in Europe, having been approved as early as 1916; however, it never had a chance to be implemented.

13. A similar, probably even worse, situation exists in other former communist countries. As Jim Podesta, an American who opened a short-lived school of journalism for 20 students in Bucharest, remarked bitterly: 'In Romania today no one understands the role of an independent, critical press. Essentially there is no journalism here. Opinion is news. Facts are dispensable': cited in Kevin Devlin, 'Postrevolutionary Ferment in the East European Media', *Radio Free Europe Report on Eastern Europe*, 13 July 1990, p.51.

14. Public opinion polls unanimously point out that the profession of journalist falls near the low end of the prestige scale, well below other intellectual professionals such as professors, teachers and doctors.

15. Norman Davies, *God's Playground: A History of Poland*, Vol 1 (Oxford: Clarendon, 1981), p.225.

16. Vincent C. Chrypinski, 'Church and Nationality in Postwar Poland', in Pedro Ramet (ed.) *Religion and Nationalism in Soviet and East European Politics* (Durham, NC: Duke University Press, 1984), p.123.

17. The legal basis is the Law on State and Church Relations approved by the communist government and parliament on 17 May 1989.

18. *Gazeta Wyborcza* 21 June 1991, p.17.

19. Ibid., 14 Sept. 1991, p.14.

20. *The New York Times*, 15 Sept. 1991, p.6, concluded that 'The Polish Roman Catholic Church lashed out at the press for what it calls distortion and "blasphemous utterances"'.

21. Prepared in May 1992; unpublished document, p.9.

22. This thesis was suggested by Rudolf Tökés, *Opposition in Eastern Europe* (London: Macmillan, 1979), pp.7–8.

23. See one such letter from the Association for Humanism and Independent Ethics, *Gazeta Wyborcza*, 12 March 1992, p.17.

24. Pál Tamás, 'Nationalism and Liberalism in the New Media Elites', unpublished paper, 1992.

25. *WV*, 30 April 1995.

26. Paolo Mancini, 'The Public Sphere and the Use of the News in a "Coalition" System of Government', in P. Dahlgreen (ed.), *Communication and Citizenship* (London: Routledge, 1991), pp.137–56.

# The Development of the Czech Media Since the Fall of Communism

## STEVE KETTLE

Despite rapid progress since the fall of communism in late 1989, much remains to be done before the media in the Czech Republic can be regarded as free and independent. In particular, attitudes instilled under communist rule influence journalists' working methods and perceptions of their role on the part of the public and politicians. Commercial pressures, including foreign investment, have led to amalgamations and closures following the mushrooming of media outlets in the early years of the decade; purges of staff and the recruitment of others by commercial media have affected quality; and the quest for popularity combined with poor professional standards as regards the checking of facts and sources leaves unanswered questions about the role of the media in the country's political life.

The Czech media have come a long way in the six years since the fall of communism in late 1989. Parallel with the rapid economic transformation of Czechoslovakia, and then the Czech Republic, towards a fully-fledged market system, the press and electronic media have been freed from heavy-handed centralized control and enjoyed the freedom to develop in a competitive environment. But there is still much to be done before the country's media can be termed genuinely free and independent.

In several respects, media professionals themselves are still struggling to define what constitutes a free press; the mentality instilled under communism continues to be evident both in their working methods and in attitudes towards the media on the part of politicians and the general public alike. Many people have found it hard to come to terms with the commercialization of the media, which has had a dramatic impact on the style of broadcasting and publications. The brashness of new tabloid papers, magazines and commercial radio and television stations initially appealed to large sections of the public as a breath of fresh air compared with the stultified and tightly controlled media of the communist era. But it shocked other sections, who feared that the country's airwaves and newsprint were being overrun by trivia and aggressive advertising. The initial surge of

Steve Kettle is a research analyst at the Open Media Research Institute, Prague. This study is based on, and expands, the same author's 'The Czech Republic Struggles to Define an Independent Press', published in *Transition* (the journal of the Open Media Research Institute), Vol.1, No.18 (6 Oct. 1995).

sensationalist programming and publications which accompanied the opening up of the media has settled down, however, in terms of audience responses: people are by now used to the new style and shape of their media.

Commercial pressures have forced the consolidation or disappearance of newspaper and magazine titles and radio stations. Many sprang up in the immediate post-communist period – far too many for their limited market. But more have survived than many experts predicted, finding their own niche and loyal audience. The immediate and continuing success of TV Nova, the first nation-wide commercial television channel to go on the air in a post-communist country, counter-balances public broadcasting and forces it to adapt its approach in the face of serious competition. The Czech Republic can boast a relatively solid and stable media spectrum. None the less, many basic questions remain about the role and functioning of the media in a still emerging democracy.

In general, journalists are well regarded by the Czech public. Opinion polls show that more respondents have faith in the media than in institutions such as the presidency, political parties, trade unions or the Catholic church. According to the state-run Institute for Public Opinion Research (IVVM), 64 per cent of respondents in a poll taken in autumn 1995 expressed trust in journalists (up from 60 per cent two years previously). President Václav Havel received a 63 per cent approval rating (61 per cent in 1993), the government 58 per cent (42 per cent), the opposition 47 per cent (35 per cent), the unions 45 per cent (43 per cent) and the church 28 per cent (26 per cent).[1]

The most serious controversies since the fall of communism over the role of the media came shortly after the break-up of Czechoslovakia. As far as most media institutions were concerned, the split of the Czech Republic and Slovakia at the end of 1992 had only a limited effect. The federalization of Czechoslovakia was the only major reform instituted during the 'Prague Spring' period led by Alexander Dubček that survived the subsequent 'normalization'. It endured the fall of communism and in many areas, including the media, was extended between 1990 and 1992 as the Czech Republic and Slovakia grew farther apart.

At the time of the split, each of the newly independent states already had its own well-developed media sector; in particular, most daily newspapers were concentrated on one or other of the two republics and there was only a limited cross-over in their circulation. Similarly, while a plethora of commercial radio stations (plus Premiéra television in the Czech Republic) existed at the time of the break-up, they were licensed for only local broadcasting and none reached the whole of Czechoslovakia. The division of the federal, public media organs – Czechoslovak Radio, Czechoslovak Television and the Czechoslovak News Agency – proved to be more difficult, and it involved changes of personnel and a change of direction. Much of the transition was achieved relatively smoothly and with services basically intact, but internal disputes led to the resignation of the director-general of Czech Radio in March 1993 after complaining of interference by the radio's supervisory board; the chairman of the board also resigned.

The Czech News Agency (ČTK) also went through a particularly turbulent period in the first half of 1993. Accusations of attempted politicization of the Czech media reached a peak in the early months of 1993, immediately after the break-up of the Czechoslovak federation. Like the division of Czechoslovakia, the media disputes can be seen as a direct consequence of the outcome of the June 1992 elections, when the Czech Republic's political focus sharpened with the victory of Prime Minister Václav Klaus's Civic Democratic Party (ODS).

The first, and most serious, controversy arose when a company that government politicians strongly objected to was granted a licence to operate the first nation-wide commercial television channel. The station finally went on the air in February 1994 as TV Nova and was an instant success. There was also a spate of other disputes between politicians and various media, and accusations that the ODS, the dominant force in the four-party governing coalition, was attempting to control or exert undue influence over the print and electronic media. Most of the Czech media can be termed right-of-centre politically, and generally supportive of the centre–right government. But the major disputes, both in the critical period in 1993 and since then, have involved Klaus and the ODS rather than left-wing opposition politicians and parties.

Censorship or any other form of direct political control does not exist in the Czech Republic. Instances of attempted manipulation of the media are, perhaps, fewer and in many cases less blatant than in other Central European countries. None the less, some professional media observers conclude that few, if any, major Czech publications can claim to be truly independent of either pressures exerted by politicians or the political and commercial interests of their owners. Part of this has been attributed to journalistic practices, the legacy of communism and ingrained habits on the part of journalists themselves.

Many who were journalists during the strictest period of 'normalization' after the Prague Spring are still active and used to propagating a pro-regime line without question. Other factors include a belief that being critical of a government that is trying to establish democracy is equivalent to an attack on the democratic process itself, and a pragmatic calculation by both journalists and publishers alike that it is better and more profitable to remain on the side of the party or group that calls the political shots.[2]

## Transition: The Written Press

One of the first laws passed by the Czechoslovak parliament in the immediate aftermath of the 'Velvet Revolution' of November 1989 guaranteed freedom of speech and of expression. A brief period of relaxation of controls had accompanied the Prague Spring, but following the invasion of Czechoslovakia by the Warsaw Pact in 1968, strict constraints were reimposed on the media; the director-general of the state news agency ČTK, his counterparts at Czechoslovak Television and Czechoslovak Radio, and other leading journalists were appointees and servants of the communist party and the government. Censorship – often, self-censorship – was tight.

The examples of the Solidarity movement in Poland and of Soviet leader Mikhail Gorbachev's policy of *glasnost* in beginning to relax restrictions on freedom of expression had little effect in Czechoslovakia. Liberal intellectuals and dissidents revived one of the leading newspapers of the pre-communist era, *Lidové noviny*, in 1988; but it appeared only monthly and in *samizdat*, as a forum for only a very tightly-knit group of people to exchange opinions and debate issues over which they could exert little or no influence. The general public was served only by publications that it did not trust.

Changes following the fall of communism initially affected newspapers more than broadcast services. The Czechoslovak Federal Assembly passed a Press Law on 28 March 1990, amending existing legislation dating back to 1966. The content and style of newspapers had already been changing rapidly in the three months since the 'Velvet Revolution' began, effectively ignoring the restrictions of the 1966 law. The revised law institutionalized these developments; it formally abolished censorship and opened the way to private ownership of publications, including ownership by foreign nationals and entities. It did not, however, address the broadcast media, where a state monopoly continued to exist.

Several dailies that existed under communist rule – and functioned as important pillars of the communist regime – continued to publish, but rapidly changed direction in order to adapt to the new circumstances. *Mladá fronta* ('Young Front'), the paper of the communist party's youth movement, the Socialist Youth Union (SSM), restored its credibility quickly by having a team of young journalists who joined in, and reported favourably on, the student-led demonstrations and other events in the hectic period of November–December 1989 that swept away communist rule. After being relaunched, the paper was renamed *Mladá fronta dnes*; over the next few years, the word *Dnes* (Today) dominated the masthead more and more while the old communist-era connotation, *Mladá fronta*, grew smaller and smaller.

*Rudé právo*, the official organ of the Central Committee of the communist party from 1921 to 1989, retained its title and format but was quickly transformed – at least, theoretically – when it was bought out by senior employees led by Zdeněk Porybný, a deputy editor under 'normalization' who became, and at the end of 1995 still remained, editor-in-chief and the driving force behind the paper's transformation. Porybný was briefly gaoled when he was accused of acting illegally in his takeover of *Rudé právo* (and its valuable printing works), but was cleared and released. The paper, while not denying its role in the communist past, was relaunched as an 'independent' daily, which is now closely allied with the opposition Social Democratic Party (ČSSD). On 18 September 1995, the daily finally got rid of the emotive word *Rudé* ('red') from its title and continued as simply *Právo* ('justice').

*Práce* ('Work'), the dull daily owned by the trade unions, continued to be supported by that source of funding, without which it would probably have folded. The unions for long resisted disposing of their 70 per cent in *Práce*, but in November 1995 agreed to sell a majority stake to a controversial businessman, Vladimír Stehlík.[3] *Lidová demokracie* ('People's Democracy'), the mouthpiece of the Czechoslovak People's Party – one of the members of the sham National Front that continued to exist under communist rule as part of the communist party's feeble attempts to demonstrate that Czechoslovakia was not just a one-party state – struggled along. It was bought from the Christian Democratic Union–Czech People's Party (KDU–CSL) in 1992 by the publisher Fidelis Schlee, but he eventually closed it down in July 1994 after the paper's circulation had fallen to around 50,000.

After the fall of communism, *Lidové noviny* ('People's News') began to publish daily on 1 April 1990 and enjoyed a surge of interest in the heady immediate aftermath of the 'Velvet Revolution'. As a trustworthy daily not only untainted by any connection with the communist past, but also a reflection of the spirit and ideals of the democratic changes, the paper peaked in the summer of 1990 when its circulation touched 400,000. The former dissidents who were the driving force behind *Lidové noviny* turned away approaches from major international media organizations and magnates such as Rupert Murdoch. But, along with its political patrons, *Lidové noviny* failed to remain in tune as the mood of the country changed from post-communist euphoria to a more hard-headed concentration on economic transformation, as reflected in the June 1992 election results. A search for investors began in early 1993; *Lidové noviny* was taken over by the Swiss group Ringier, many senior staff left the paper and its circulation subsequently slipped drastically.

## Ownership of the Press: Foreign Influence

A lack of domestic funds and know-how determined that the transformation and modernization of the Czech press would have to be financed and directed largely from abroad. By mid-1994, it was calculated that more than 50 per cent of the Czech press was foreign-owned, with at least 16 of the 25 biggest daily publications in foreign hands. Regional dailies were sold off to publishing houses, mainly from neighbouring Austria and Germany. Hans Kapfinger GmbH, a sister company of the Neue Passauer Presse group based in Bavaria, acquired more than 25 titles and was the subject of anti-monopoly investigations: on 29 June 1993 the Ministry for Economic Co-operation banned the proposed merger of 11 titles in the group's Czech holdings. The Ringier group, which made its debut with the financial weekly *Profit* in 1990, took the Czech market by storm when it launched the raunchy tabloid *Blesk* ('Lightning') in 1992; it quickly became the biggest-selling daily in the Czech Republic. By the end of 1992, *Blesk* sold an average of 500,000 copies daily compared with 360,000 for the second most widely read, *Mladá fronta dnes*; a year later, it had cornered 24.4 per cent of the daily market, while *Mladá fronta dnes*'s market share was 16.6 per cent and third-placed *Rudé právo* had 13 per cent.[4] Ringier also bought a majority stake in *Lidové noviny* in November 1993 and has established three printing centres.

The most successful of the mid-market or serious dailies, *Mladá fronta dnes*, became part of the Socpresse empire owned by the French media magnate Robert Hersant, until Hersant ran into serious financial difficulties. In December 1994, the German Rheinisch–Bergische group, based in Düsseldorf, took over 74 per cent of Socpresse's majority stake in the holding company which controls *Mladá fronta dnes* and the weekly magazine *Respekt*. Other foreign-owned or -controlled publications include Czech versions of best-selling international titles such as *Playboy*, *Elle*, *PC World* and *Reader's Digest*, all of which have established themselves successfully in the Czech market. Among the three biggest-selling dailies, only *Rudé právo* (now *Právo*) remained in domestic hands.

Czechs are relatively avid newspaper readers; for a population of 10.5 million, the 10 biggest-selling national dailies between them sell just under one million copies daily, according to the May 1995 audit by the Daily Newspaper Publishers' Association. *Blesk*'s extraordinary initial success has tailed off: in May 1995, *Mladá fronta dnes* sold an average of 348,000 copies daily and *Rudé právo* almost 275,000, while *Blesk* was down to third place with just under 270,000. According to another survey, *Mladá fronta dnes*'s sales translated into a total readership of 1.3 million, *Blesk*'s to 1.2 million and *Rudé právo*'s to 800,000. Seven papers sell an average of more than 100,000 copies a day, with the farmers' daily *Zemédelské noviny* in fourth place, the economic *Hospodářské noviny* fifth, the left-of-centre *Svobodné slovo* sixth and the popular tabloid *Expres*, seventh.[5]

A wide range of dailies and weeklies still exists and commercial pressures have forced the closure of only a few, such as *Lidová demokracie*. The right-wing *Český deník* ('Czech Daily') has turned into a weekly (*Český týdeník*) instead of appearing daily. Other right-wing papers have merged: in 1992, *Telegraf* absorbed *Metropolitán*, and four months later also took over the short-lived *Prostor* ('Outlook'), and later became *Denní Telegraf* ('Daily Telegraph'). The publishers of *Denní Telegraf*, which is tainted with being seen as the house organ of Prime Minister Klaus's ODS, did not provide figures for the May 1995 survey, but its circulation has been estimated at less than 40,000.[6] In eighth place, *Práce* sells almost 88,000 copies daily – ahead of ninth-ranked *Lidové noviny* and *Sport*, which is in tenth place.

### Transition: The Broadcast Media

Following the Press Law of March 1990, and the general election in June of that year, the government of Czechoslovakia turned its attention to the broadcast media. A policy declaration made to parliament included a promise to introduce pluralism in radio and television, and in the period 1991–92 four broadcasting laws were adopted either by the Czechoslovak Federal Assembly or by the Czech and Slovak regional parliaments (then called national councils). The Law on Radio and Television Broadcasting adopted by the Federal Assembly on 30 October 1991 continues to form the basis for electronic media activities in the Czech Republic. It abolished the state monopoly on broadcasting and provided for a dual system whereby public and private operators would coexist.[7] A nine-member Federal Broadcasting Council was created as the body authorized to issue radio and television licences to private operators and supervise broadcast operations. The Council consisted of three members nominated by the Czechoslovak Federal Assembly, three by the Czech National Council and three by the Slovak National Council. By a law passed by the Czech National Council on 21 February 1992, a Board for Radio and Television Broadcasting for the Czech Republic was created, which took the place of the federal Council after the split of Czechoslovakia. Its constitution and duties remained the same, but its nine members were appointed solely by the Czech parliament, raising doubts about how independently it could operate or whether it would only serve particular political interests.

Under the 1992 law, the board is officially an independent body accountable only to the parliament. The members, elected for a six-year term, are barred from holding official posts in any political party or in the management of media concerns; they may not have any financial interest in broadcasting companies or any other commercial interests that could affect their decisions. As well as issuing and revoking radio and television broadcasting licences, the board is charged with ensuring that broadcasting laws are being complied with and helping to determine state broadcasting policies.[8] Separate, individual boards supervise the actual functioning of the public sector broadcasters, Czech Radio and Czech Television; they, too are responsible to parliament and, among other functions, appoint or recall the director-general of each organization.

Granting local licences for commercial radio broadcasters stirred up little controversy, and the first commercial television station – Premiéra, which was set up with the help of Italian investors – went on the air in June 1993, broadcasting to Prague and parts of South Bohemia. But on 30 January 1993, the board unanimously voted to grant the first nation-wide licence for a television channel to a group called CET 21 (Central European Television for the 21st Century). The new station – which became TV Nova – would broadcast on the channel previously used by Czechoslovak Television for its main channel and subsequently taken over (in the Czech Republic) by Czech Television. Among CET 21's principals were two who had been active in politics as leading figures in liberal groups that lost power in the June 1992 general election: Fedor Gál, former chairman of the (Slovak) Public Against Violence movement, and Vladimír Železný, former spokesman of the (Czech) Civic Movement and of Klaus's predecessor as Czech prime minister, Petr Pithart. At the time it granted the licence, the Board for Radio and Television Broadcasting had only six members; three Slovak members who had served *ex officio* until the splitting of Czechoslovakia four weeks earlier had not yet been replaced; the remaining six had all been appointed before the June 1992 elections.

Moreover, CET 21 was backed by foreign capital. A 22 per cent stake was held by the Czech state savings bank, Česká Spořitelna, but the majority financing (66 per cent) came from the Berlin-based Central European Development Corporation (CEDC), headed by the former US ambassador to Hungary, Mark Palmer, and underwritten by the heir to the Estee Lauder cosmetics fortune, Ronald Lauder. The Board's decision was taken after a process of open competition, in which the more than 20 unsuccessful bidders included domestic groups and European media giants such as the German Bertlesmann group and Italian tycoon Silvio Berlusconi.

According to the 1991 broadcasting law, the Board for Radio and Television Broadcasting was obliged to take into consideration many factors when issuing licences. Licensed companies must comply with the law's provisions on the amount of time allowed for commercials, and news programmes may not have commercial sponsors. The licence holder must broadcast programmes to serve the 'public interest', contribute to the 'strengthening of democracy' and 'reflect pluralism of opinions', and must not propagate a particular religious group or political orientation or support a particular political group.[9] After the decision was announced, the board's chairman, Daniel Korte, said it had followed the criteria laid down in the law and chosen CET 21 'simply because its proposal was better than that of other companies' and CET 21 had demonstrated that it had sufficient, reliable financial backing. Železný, who became TV Nova's director-general, said that CEDC (operating through Central European Media Enterprises, or CME) would not influence CET 21's proposed programming and promised that the company would be politically independent.[10]

Klaus's ODS party immediately issued a statement terming the board's choice of CET 21 'politically dangerous' and calling on the Czech parliament to tackle this 'serious problem'. The statement named Gál, Železný and Palmer in its attacks and suggested that CET 21, because of the personalities involved, would have a pro-Slovak and anti-Hungarian bias. Klaus said the awarding of the licence was 'an incredibly strange decision'.[11] The executive deputy chairman of the ODS, Petr Čermák, went much further in a newspaper interview. He said he would do 'everything in my power' to overturn the board's decision and 'I absolutely cannot accept that the main news medium, which is what television is, should be in the hands of failed politicians who are not only the cause of many of the problems we currently face but are, moreover, from Slovakia'. Čermák also derided Palmer and called the board's decision 'a basic threat to democracy and perhaps to the foundations of this state'.[12]

President Václav Havel joined in the dispute by reprimanding Čermák. Referring to the jibe about 'failed politicians', Havel said: 'I know this concept well. It was used by communist propaganda for decades.'[13] Despite attempts from ODS deputies to have the board dismissed, on 3 February the parliament instead filled the three vacancies on the board; six days later, all nine members unanimously approved specific conditions that CET 21 must meet, effectively reconfirming its licensing decision. The passions aroused over the CET 21 affair can be partially explained by the fact that the awarding of licences by the Board for Radio and Television Broadcasting to commercial companies amounts to a privatization process, as it involves frequencies and assets previous held by public corporations, Czech Television and Czech Radio. As such, the process can have far-reaching political consequences which the small and inexperienced board may not be able to foresee or deal with. However, the fury over CET 21 was not repeated less than one month later when the board issued two licences for nation-wide radio stations, taking FM channels from Czech Radio. One licence was issued to a company formed by two local music-based stations already operating in the Czech Republic, Radio Golem and Radio Evropa 2, the latter being an offshoot of the French commercial station Europe 2.

Offering a mixture of pop music, news and magazine-style current affairs programmes, this station was named Freqvence 1.

The second licence was awarded to a newcomer, Radio Alfa, which was headed by a group of experienced radio and print journalists who promised to focus their programming on broadcasting news and analysis. Radio Alfa became the first nation-wide commercial broadcaster totally financed from domestic Czech sources when it went on the air on 13 October 1993, one month before Freqvence 1. But even before it started as a serious challenger to Czech Radio's flagship Radiožurnál station, Alfa lost one of its principal founders to TV Nova and it soon ran into difficulties (see below). Although some of the 16 companies who bid unsuccessfully for the radio licences complained about the decisions, Korte said the Board was not subjected to political pressure during the decision-making process or afterwards, in direct contrast to the case of CET 21. None the less, Korte resigned on 27 May 1993, complaining of political interference in the work of the board and accusing Klaus and some parliamentary deputies of favouring greater government control over the media.[14]

Under new leadership, the board in April 1994 ignored objections from the parliamentary media committee and issued a licence to Radio Echo to broadcast a news-based station on a medium-wave frequency previously used by Czech Radio's Radiožurnál. But three months later, the parliament voted by a large majority to sack the entire board after rejecting its annual report, noting in particular the board's failure to justify why the second channel of Czech Television, ČT2, should not be privatized.[15]

### Transition: Česká Tisková Kancelář (ČTK)

The heads of the major public-owned media – Czech Television, Czech Radio and the news agency ČTK – are appointed by supervisory boards responsible to parliament, but only in the latter case have there been accusations of attempted political control. The general director of Czech Television, Ivo Mathé, is a professional television producer who has spent all his career since 1976 in television, remaining non-partisan. Vlastimil Ježek, appointed to run Czech Radio from July 1993, won an open competition for the post despite having only a brief journalistic background; he too, however, has never belonged to any political party although he campaigned for the liberal Civic Movement in the 1992 elections.

ČTK (Československá tisková kancelář until 1992, before it was divided up when the Czech Republic and Slovakia split) was, in the past, the major media tool of the communist party, holding a near-monopoly on distributing information to the rest of the domestic media and abroad. In the eyes of some politicians and officials, ČTK should continue to be a conduit for transmitting official statements, rather than an independent agency operating unfettered and exercising its own editorial control. The seven members of ČTK's supervisory board may not hold a post in a political party nor use their position in the council to act in the interests of any particular party. But while Czech Television and Czech Radio are largely funded through licence fees and advertising revenue, ČTK's dependence on direct subsidies from the state budget for much of its financing makes it particularly vulnerable to political interference. In turn, most of the Czech media are heavily dependent on ČTK for their news.

All three state-owned media organs were heavily purged of personnel following the fall of communism, taken out of government control and transformed into public service entities. Under amendments passed in 1991 to the 1965 law establishing and defining the activities of ČTK, the agency was no longer considered to be an 'official' mouthpiece. Henceforth, ČTK was conjoined only to provide objective and balanced information for the free expression of opinions.

The first post-communist director-general of ČTK was Petr Uhl, a left-wing journalist and dissident who served nine years in jail under the communist regime. After the victory of the ODS in the June 1992 elections, he was replaced in September of that year by Tomáš Kopřiva, a former journalist on a Christian magazine and an ODS member of the federal parliament until the elections. Uhl had also been a federal parliament deputy; both were elected in 1990 for the Civic Forum, but, when this broke up, Uhl joined the Civic Movement that was trounced by the ODS in the 1992 elections. Before Kopriva's arrival, ČTK had already lost a large number of experienced staff, who left to join the plethora of media outlets that had emerged since November 1989.

Under Kopřiva's leadership, dozens more threatened to quit, claiming that they were being forced to work according to political, rather than editorial, criteria and that the agency was being run unprofessionally.[16] Kopriva dismissed editor-in-chief Petr Holubec after he expressed a lack of confidence in the director-general, but ČTK's debilitating internal crisis began to be resolved only when Kopriva was replaced in June 1993 by Milan Stibral, a journalist with long service at ČTK who hitherto had been in charge of the agency's photographic services. Stibral reinstated Holubec but, in the meantime, members of the Daily Newspaper Publishers' Association had decided they no longer had faith in ČTK and established their own rival news agency, Česká tisková agentura (ČTA).

### Politicians and the Media: Journalistic Standards

The CET 21 affair showed a clear lack of respect among some politicians for the independence of the media. Further incidents prompted even government supporters in the media to be critical of the attitude of government politicians. In early 1993, ODS deputies proposed in parliament that a monopoly on the distribution of publications should be reestablished, claiming that some newspapers were not available in some outlets and a monopoly distributor would be able to ensure that all readers would have access to the paper of their choice. The proposal, seen as an attempt to promote papers that supported the government, came to nought, but further incidents intensified feelings among journalists that the media were under constant sniper attack from politicians.

The major clash following the CET 21 affair arose in September 1994, with charges that Klaus and ODS deputy chairman Čermák were instrumental in forcing the editor-in-chief of *Telegraf*, Pavel Šafr, to resign for publishing articles critical of the government. In an attempt to boost the paper's flagging circulation, Šafr had changed the direction of *Telegraf* from its previous close association with the ODS; the daily's majority shareholder, the state-owned Investiční a poštovní banka, objected – under pressure from Čermák, Šafr alleged on television.[17] He resigned, along with 17 other senior journalists, and was replaced by Viktor Krejčí, whose previous task was to conduct interviews with Klaus and write pro-government editorials.[18] Both Klaus and Čermák denied any involvement in Šafr's removal, but the mud stuck. *Mladá fronta dnes*, which is generally favourable towards the government, ran an editorial saying that the ODS was behaving towards the media like a 'bull in a china shop'. The editorial warned ODS leaders that attempted pressure on the media by political leaders generally ended with the politicians themselves being discredited.[19]

Klaus's own attitude towards the media was illustrated by a now celebrated remark that 'journalists are the biggest enemies of mankind'. The comment was made at the end of an interview with Forbes magazine in 1994; Klaus believed his words were off the record, not part of the interview, and complained that it was unprofessional journalism for the remark to be reported and then also widely picked up by other publications. At the end of May 1994, Klaus cut short an interview with TV Nova when he objected to aggressive questioning by the interviewer, Luboš Beniak. Nova management withdrew the interview before its scheduled broadcast slot, claiming its technical quality was too poor for the interview to be aired. For one whose contempt for journalists is expressed frequently, however, Klaus commands more space in newspapers than many staff professionals. His weekly column in *Lidové noviny*, which is also carried by some regional newspapers, plus at least one interview a week in the same paper, have been cited as reasons why *Lidové noviny* has lost tens of its reporters, writers and editors in the past year. Some left, complaining that the paper had lost its long-standing tradition as a liberal organ critical of the establishment since the Ringier takeover.

Questions were also raised, this time by members of other parties in the governing coalition, when TV Nova offered Klaus a five-minute weekly spot to answer viewers' questions and comments. The programme went on the air in September 1995; the other parties objected that, with less than nine months to go before a scheduled general election, Klaus would use it to further his own party's electoral chances. According to Nova, the programme quickly became one of its most popular offerings, with an audience of 1.5 million, but Nova management still had to decide whether to continue the programme beyond its originally planned run, due to end in March 1996, little more than two months before the elections.[20]

Klaus has also attacked state-run Czech Television, on one occasion protesting that only snippets of an 'important' speech he made were broadcast.[21] The director of Czech Television apologized and said his news staff had made a mistake. ODS leaders also complained in early 1995 that ČTK failed to publish in full a statement by the head of the secret service concerning a scandal raging at the time over alleged spying on political parties by the service. ODS and other politicians introduced into the parliament draft legislation which would force ČTK to publish, unedited and in full, statements by public and government functionaries.[22]

In reply, ČTK editor-in-chief Petr Holubec said that 'ČTK's service should stem from the needs of the media, not those of politicians, and the solution is to privatize the agency with media involvement and abolish the law on ČTK'.[23] Klaus has several times complained that ČTK edits down and distorts his pronouncements, but the government finally decided in March that there was no need to revise the law which governs the establishment and operation of ČTK – meaning that there are no immediate plans to privatize the agency.

Despite the ODS's clashes with some sections of the media, the opposition leader Miloš Zeman has repeatedly charged the Czech press with being servile towards the government.[24] Czech Television's news reporting remains largely passive and formalistic, with many journalists delivering ponderous reports in a machine-gun monotone as if reading out official proclamations. Nova, while frequently sensationalistic and 'tabloid' and less geared than the state-owned channel to handling hard foreign news, none the less also includes a more aggressive and investigative approach, challenging officials and other subjects of their reports and often treading on their toes.

In the written press, well-rounded and comprehensive articles which examine official policies and attitudes in depth, rather than simply accepting them at face value or blindly attacking them, are rare. The weekly *Respekt* is the notable exception, but other former news magazines have gone down-market to resemble the gossip publications that dominate the magazine market. The background research and preparation of articles continues to be weak or absent in much of the Czech press, often leaving readers to work out for themselves the relevance of a report; many newspapers can be justifiably criticized for presenting articles based on the author's opinions rather than facts. Reprinting ČTK reports verbatim, without attempts to take them further or even tailor the style to that of individual newspapers, is still widespread.

Among journalists, media watchers and even some politicians who strongly oppose its past or current politics, *Právo* is often considered to be the most professional daily for the breadth and directness of its news reporting; there is less obfuscation than in other papers. Among readers, *Právo*'s past history and role as a major pillar of communist rule still engenders resistance to it, and some of its treatment of sensitive topics, such as the Sudeten German issue, or crimes committed by members of the Romany community, can give it a sometimes xenophobic flavour.

Many officials and public figures are unaccustomed to dealing with an inquisitive press, and often refuse to do so. The director-general of SPT Telecom, the state-controlled telecommunications company and one of the Czech Republic's largest industrial concerns, objected to articles in *Mladá fronta dnes* about his firm and demanded that future articles could only appear with his express permission and agreement on their content.[25] The official concerned, Jiří Makovec, was fired shortly afterwards, his attitude towards the media being cited as a factor in his dismissal.[26]

Less than fully professional reporting leaves journalists and publications open to legal action, and a string of libel suits is constantly before the courts. Parliamentary committees since April have been discussing the possibility of making it obligatory for papers to print the replies of people whose are quoted or mentioned in articles. Journalists complain that this would lead to a ridiculous situation: a politician could refuse to give information requested by a journalist, would have the right to reply to an article that nevertheless appeared on the subject – but even in his reply, the politician would still be able to withhold facts relevant to the article.[27]

On 18 October 1995, the government approved a draft law that would deprive journalists of the right to protect their sources and no longer require government institutions to provide information to journalists. Both provisions were contained in the original draft submitted by the minister of culture, Pavel Tigrid, but were removed in the full Cabinet session. Klaus and other supporters of the government version argued that journalists should be given no special privileges and that all citizens have the right under existing Czech law to information.[28]

Deputy Prime Minister Jan Kalvoda, leader of the Civic Democratic Alliance, distanced himself from the government's decision, saying journalists should have the right to protect their sources; opposition leader Zeman accused the ODS, which has a majority in the government and can outvote its coalition partners, of trying to limit press freedom ahead of the campaign for the general election due in mid-1996.[29] Critics within the media charged that the bill was a 'bastard', serving no one's interests and demonstrating the inability of politicians to understand the concept of freedom of information.[30]

## Consolidation of the Broadcast Media

TV Nova began broadcasting on 4 February 1994. In the year between CET 21 being granted its licence and the launch of the new station, Nova ran a huge advertising campaign directed against the existing public broadcaster; one advert proclaimed, 'We are Czech television, not Czech Television'. A strongly antagonistic relationship with Czech Television has continued ever since. The launch of Nova was not without its problems; leading members of its news team left shortly before the station went on the air, but Nova made an immediate impact with its diet of imported soap operas, game shows and films. Premiéra had already been widely criticized for its reliance on cheap imports; Nova promised more Czech-made programmes, almost all commissioned from independent producers. According to the terms of its licence, domestically produced programmes had to form at least 25 per cent of Nova's programming at the outset, rising to more than 50 per cent within five years. The success or failure of Nova, representing the first major breakthrough in bringing open competition in television, was widely seen as a touchstone for opening up the broadcasting media throughout Central and Eastern Europe.

Within weeks of being launched, Nova superseded Czech Television's 'mass audience' channel, ČT1, as the most popular television station. In the first quarter of 1994, Nova claimed 49.6 per cent of the viewing audience, compared with 38.2 per cent for ČT1, 4.1 per cent for ČT2, and 3.4 per cent for Premiéra. The initial surge was then extended: at the end of 1994, Nova had 68.4 per cent, ČT1 24.2 per cent, ČT2 2.3 per cent and Premiéra 1.7 per cent. In May 1995, Nova claimed a 70.4 per cent market share, with ČT1 tailing off further at 22.2 per cent, ČT2 on 3.2 per cent and Premiéra 1.4 per cent.[31] Although a popular success, Nova has continued to claim that Czech Television still has an unfair commercial advantage from licence fee revenues and has urged that the amount of advertising on the public stations should be reduced. Nova is permitted to use ten per cent of air time on commercials, ČT1 one per cent and ČT2 seven per cent. Czech Television's director general, Ivo Mathé, refuted the challenge, saying that advertising provides Czech Television with only 0.5 billion crowns of its budget of three billion crowns; licence fees cover two billion crowns, and the rest is made up from the company's reserves and from selling programmes; Nova's income from advertising, meanwhile, is estimated at three billion crowns, making it already on a par with Czech Television.[32]

A further challenge to Czech Television comes from Premiéra. Its transmitters currently reach about half of the Czech Republic, but the station has suffered severe financial problems from the outset. According to press reports, it lost 107 million crowns in 1994[33] and its majority owner, Investiční a poštovní banka, has been seeking new investors for more than a year. Among the most recent possible candidates to take over Premiéra are two American groupings, one made up of Turner Broadcasting and Time Warner and the other ABC and Disney.[34] In the meantime, Premiéra is seeking to extend its broadcasting area by securing frequencies currently operated by ČT2, Czech Television's minority or 'cultural' channel. The channel was leased to Czech Television only until the end of 1995: ČT2's future, and the desirable balance between public and commercial broadcasting, have been keenly debated but, at the time of writing, no decision had been made.

Like TV Nova, the two original nation-wide radio channels made a good start. Freqvence 1 established itself alongside Czech Radio's Radiožurnál as a middle-of-the-road 'family' station mixing news, music and magazine programmes. By the end of September 1995, it claimed 15.68 per cent of the total audience with more than 1.1 million listeners daily, comparable to Radiožurnál's figures.[35] Radio Alfa, however, ran into financial problems and internal difficulties led to a loss of staff, including two of its senior journalists moving to help found Radio Echo. In November 1994 the Board for Radio and Television Broadcasting refused a request by Alfa to allow Central European Media Enterprises (CME) – the company with a controlling interest in TV Nova – to take a substantial stake in the station, ruling that it would create a monopolistic situation in the commercial media sector. Despite this, Alfa announced a new format in September 1995 and began broadcasting as Radio Nova Alfa, sharing some programme presenters with the television station and concentrating on pop music programming.

The board declared that Alfa was not adhering to the terms of its licence, which stipulated that it was a news and current affairs channel; on 8 November 1995, it imposed a one-million-crown fine when Alfa did not return to its original format, which allows a maximum of 45 per cent music. The Board again refused to allow CME to take a 28 per cent stake in Alfa. At the same session, the board revoked Radio Echo's licence. The station started broadcasting in July 1994, but it failed to secure a foothold in the market. Echo's founders quickly lost control to the station's two major investors – the Bonton group, which includes the Radio Bonton music radio station in Prague, and Investiční a poštovní banka – but they later pulled out.

Radio Echo went off the air on 31 July 1995 and remained silent until the board withdrew its licence. The experience of Radio Echo was termed an 'unsuccessful hybrid of a commercial and a "cultural" station'.[36] Despite the commercial difficulties faced by many local radio stations, few others have so far gone to the wall. Many are operated on a shoestring, and listener figures of 10,000 are considered a success. But the board, reviewing the licences of the 13 commercial stations operating in Prague which expire at the end of 1995, decided to renew all but four, two of which had already ceased broadcasting because of lack of finance.[37]

## Conclusion

The Czech media, in keeping with the general trends in the country, have developed along free-market but essentially pragmatic lines since 1989. Few formal restrictions exist on the written press: the 1990 Press Law allows anyone to start a publication, simply by registering it. Otherwise, publishers merely have to abide by existing laws. The new freedoms have changed the media landscape dramatically in the past six years, but have also made room for a proliferation of pornography and sensationalism. However, a magazine that published a series of anti-Semitic pieces, *Politika*, was shut down in 1992 and its publisher prosecuted on charges of spreading racial hatred.[38] Conflicts with owners over editorial control of publications, with or without outside political interference, have of course occurred. In October 1993, the editor-in-chief of *Český deník* resigned, accusing its publisher, Josef Kudláček, of constantly interfering in editorial decisions and preferring right-wing polemics to balanced journalism. At the time of Ringier's takeover of *Lidové noviny*, the paper's editor-in-chief, Jaromír Štětina, wrote an editorial to calm fears that the Swiss owners would transform the paper along the lines of its new tabloid stablemate, *Blesk*. Two months later, Štětina resigned, giving as his reason editorial interference by Ringier, and sparked off a mass exodus of staff.[39]

Commercial considerations have also played an inevitable part in the way the Czech media have developed. In the period from 1990 to 1994, the advertising market rose spectacularly: for the written press, from 0.25 billion crowns annually to 3.8 billion, for radio 0.1 billion to 0.6 billion and for television, 0.1 billion to 2.7 billion.[40] The boom in advertising revenues has allowed, and determined, that the Czech press sinks or swims according to market forces; with the sale of *Práce* to a private publisher, the last of the major Czech dailies that had been kept alive by subsidies from a particular interest group will also be subject to free commercial competition.

Both the written press and the electronic media have had to feel their way tentatively in rapidly changing conditions, with no previous experience to fall back on. Shortcomings of journalistic training are still widely apparent and journalists themselves can be justifiably accused of mixing unsubstantiated assertions or their own opinions in with facts; they are often unable to remain above politics and a particular ideology influences their work, leading to bias and incomplete reporting.

In that sense, should the government's proposed revised Press Law pass on to the statute book, the media will have to accept that the new requirements are, in part, a result of their own flawed professional standards. On the other hand, open reporting of a string of political scandals has both tested journalists' investigative skills and demonstrated their growing ability to challenge the political establishment. Many politicians have not come to terms with the existence or desirability of genuinely free media in their country, still seeing the need for political control. The parliamentary media committee acts as a political watchdog, but with few formal powers except in the legislative field. The written press is not subjected to any direct supervision, but the Board for Radio and Television Broadcasting can be used as a political tool. After it was disbanded in July 1994, the board was reconstituted on lines of party affiliation rather than according to the qualifications and expertise of its individual members.[41] Despite concerns, however, the sweeping changes since 1989 – especially the conflicts and mistakes – have provided a body of experience for the further positive development of the Czech media along free and independent lines.

## NOTES

1. See *Lidové noviny*, 20 Oct. 1995.
2. See Jiří Hanák, 'Noviny a novináři', in *KMIT* (Komunikace, Média, Informacé, Technologie), 1995, No.5.
3. *Právo* and *Hospodářské noviny*, 28 Nov. 1995.
4. Figures from AISA. See *Rudé právo*, 17 Nov. 1993.
5. Media Projekt '95. See *Mladá fronta dnes*, 3 and 11 Aug. 1995.
6. *Prague Post*, 7 Sept. 1994.
7. See Frank L. Kaplan and Milan Šmíd, 'Broadcasting in Czechoslovakia and the Czech Republic after 1989: Overhauling the System and its Structures', *Javnost*, Vol.2, No.3 (1995), pp.33–45.
8. See Jiří Pehe, 'Furor over Independent Radio and Television', *RFE/RL Research Report*, 9 April 1993.
9. Ibid.
10. ČTK, 1 Feb. 1993.
11. *Hospodářské noviny*, 2 Feb. 1993.

12. *Telegraf*, 2 Feb. 1993.
13. *Mladá fronta dnes*, 3 Feb. 1993.
14. *RFE/RL Daily Report*, 28 May 1993.
15. *Mladá fronta dnes*, 11 July 1994.
16. *RFE/RL Daily Report*, 8 April 1993.
17. ČT1, 1 Sept. 1994.
18. See *Prague Post*, 7 Sept. 1994 and *Frankfurter Allgemeine Zeitung*, 14 Sept. 1994.
19. *Mladá fronta dnes*, 7 Sept. 1994.
20. *Lidové noviny*, 22 Nov. 1995.
21. *Mladá fronta dnes*, 17 Sept. 1993.
22. *Rudé právo*, 1 Feb. 1995.
23. Open Media Research Institute, *Daily Digest*, 2 Feb. 1995.
24. See, for example, *Rudé právo*, 19 Sept. 1994.
25. *Mladá fronta dnes*, 15 Dec. 1994.
26. See Steve Kettle, 'Foreign Investment and the SPT Telecom Deal', in *Transition*, 22 Sept. 1995.
27. *Mladá fronta dnes*, 5 April 1995.
28. Open Media Research Institute, *Daily Digest*, 20 Oct. 1995.
29. *Právo*, 21 Oct. 1995.
30. *Respekt*, 23 Nov. 1995.
31. Media Projekt '95; also, Kaplan and Šmíd, 'Broadcasting in Czechoslovakia'.
32. *Lidové noviny*, 11 Nov. 1995.
33. *Rudé právo*, 20 April 1995.
34. *Mladá fronta dnes*, 20 Oct. 1995.
35. Media Projekt '95.
36. *Respekt*, 18 Sept. 1995.
37. *Lidové noviny*, 15 Nov. 1995.
38. See Jiří Pehe, 'Media in Eastern Europe: The Czech Republic', in RFE/RL Research Report 7 May 1993.
39. Reuters, 11 Jan. 1994.
40. *Lidové noviny*, 15 April 1995.
41. See Kaplan and Šmíd, 'Broadcasting in Czechoslovakia'.

# Journalists, Political Elites and the Post-Communist Public: The Case of Slovakia

## ANDREJ ŠKOLKAY

In the period since the collapse of communism (which included the establishment of Slovakia as an independent state), there have been significant changes in the media institutions in the country, but the absence of an established civil society has made the media vulnerable to attempts at political control. State involvement remains particularly high in the broadcasting media. Lack of clarity has characterized legislation on the media, and financial and other pressure has been applied to media deemed hostile to the government. The involvement of leading media figures in politics further undermines the independence of communications media. There is serious debate about the proper role of mass media in the process of building democracy, and in a polarized society it seems clear that government influence will remain for some time to come.

This contribution describes and analyses the development of relations between journalists and politicians in post-communist Slovak society during the six years since the overthrow of communism. It offers an overview of changes in media institutions and the attempts of post-communist political elites to gain control over the mass media, subordinating public opinion to will of the government. Although such endeavours are not unusual in other post-communist countries, the present article contributes to the discussion in this area. In particular, the Slovak case is instructive in that it analyses the role of independent state and governmental institutions in guaranteeing an autonomous public media system, and how its absence or weakness allows for intervention into media content by political elites. In general, it appears that these actions are closely related to the weakness of civil society, which is unable to check the expansion of elite power and its encroachment on mass communications.

## Media Institutions and their Function under State Socialism

As might be expected, the role of the media in East European societies

Andrej Školkay is an instructor and doctoral candidate in the Department of Political Science at the Comenius University, Bratislava. This work was supported by the Research Support Scheme of the Higher Education Support Programme, grant No.324/1995.

reflected both the ideological dictates of Marxism-Leninism and the practical objectives of political leaders from state to state. In accordance with Lenin's theory of the press, mass communications in communist societies served as a clear tool of partisanship, reinforcing ideological norms.[1] Leninist views of the press, combined with the theoretical supremacy of Marxist-Leninist philosophy and the needs of totalitarian regimes to influence public opinion, led to censorship in its various forms across communist states. Thus, the suppression of press freedom was among first steps of communist regimes in Bolshevik Russia and Eastern Europe, although in Central and East European countries this was often an incremental process. This is particularly true with regard to Czechoslovakia.[2]

## The Czechoslovak Media, 1948–89

In the first years of communist rule in Czechoslovakia there was no formal press censorship. The communist government was able to manage the media through those within the press who were either party members or sympathizers, and also through their influence in the Union of Journalists, which had a great deal of legal power. Most importantly, during this early period there was a significant degree of unity between the government, communist journalists and a large segment of the public.[3] Nevertheless, upon coming to power in February 1948, the communist party radically reduced the number of published dailies, a goal achieved by a combination of administrative and political pressure.[4] With power firmly established, a new system of press control was developed.[5]

One of the most important institutions was the Central Authority of Press Supervision, established in 1953 to conduct media censorship. This office existed under various names until spring 1990, with the exception of a three-month period during the Prague Spring of 1968. Other controls were established through vertical lines of authority and the *nomenklatura*. For example, in the area of the electronic media, until 1959 directors of central radio and television channels were nominated by the central government, while directors of regional radio and television channels in Slovakia were elected by the presidium of the Slovak parliament on the proposal of central directors. In this way overlapping lines of control were established not only from central institutions but also through local communist power structures. After federalization in 1969 regional directors were nominated by the presidium of the Slovak parliament on the proposal of the cabinet, although both institutions remained subordinate to federal broadcasting institutions.

Beginning in 1953 and lasting until 1966, press control took the form of 'pre-censorship': control over press content prior to its publication. In January 1967 a new law came into effect. Under this law, while the office of censorship (now known as the Central Publishing Authority) retained the right to stop the publication or distribution of state information, economic or other 'official secrets', it granted, at least in theory, the final decision in such matters to the courts. With regard to less sensitive information (the publication of which would be considered against the interests of society) the censors could only inform the editor-in-chief and publisher, who were authorized to make a final decision.

However, owing to the power of the *nomenklatura* and the weak protests of publishers and editors, censorship remained as a *de facto* instrument of central control. Ironically, it was this law that finally legalized censorship, since the existence of the previous office of censorship had in fact been a violation of the law.[6] Continuing struggles by journalists eventually led to the wider publication of more reformist ideas, although these remained within a clearly socialist framework. After the changes in party leadership in early 1968 *de facto* censorship ceased to exist, but shortly after the intervention by armies of the Warsaw Pact (excluding Romania) this law was annulled and press controls were reinstated. The importance of secrecy and pre-censorship during the 1960s is demonstrated by the fact that there existed no fewer than nine different directives relating to specific kinds of censorship and the classification of information as state secrets.[7]

As a result of changes in the press law of 1966, editors theoretically had relatively more freedom in decision-making. According to the new law censorship extended only to 'politically incorrect' articles or programmes, placing much of the authority in the hands of individual censors and the media themselves. However, strict censorship remained until the first months of 1968, since, as was often the case, the communist leadership did not respect its own laws. Theoretically there even existed the possibility for journalists to turn to the courts in case of such disputes, but this was widely recognized as unlikely. Even so, most editors, being themselves party members, respected the 'recommendations' of state censors during this short period between 1966 and 1968. There were, however, two important exceptions: the weekly publications of Slovak and Czech writers, *Kultúrny život* ('Cultural Life') in Slovakia and *Literarni noviny* ('Literary Newspaper') in the Czech Lands, were the only papers 'that the powers-that-be had not managed to get under their control, officially or otherwise'.[8] This was true until end of 1967, when *Literarni noviny* was not re-registered as an official publication with the Union of Czechoslovak Writers.

This struggle was not entirely in vain, at least in the short term. Censorship in Czechoslovakia eventually broke down under the continuous pressure of more daring editors and printers. In early March 1968 the newspaper *Práce* bypassed censors and published an article about the defection of an army general who had been under criminal investigation, a former protégé of the head of state. This independent action served as a catalyst, effectively undermining censorship power; as one observer put it, 'in a few days, the agents of censorship who had for years been working in shifts around the clock on each newspaper, radio and television station quietly walked away'.[9] This *de facto* situation became *de jure* some four months later, when an official law abolishing censorship was passed by parliament.

After the crushing of Prague Spring in 1968, a new and more efficient kind of censorship was enacted, with supervising offices at the federal, republican and regional levels engaged in 'post-censorship', or the monitoring of what had already been disseminated in the media. Top offices had broad legal powers that included not only financial sanctions but also the ability to suspend the publication of newspapers or magazines for up to three months. The practice of post-censorship developed additional facets as well. Possible sanctions were linked through publishers to their editors; editors-in-chief therefore sought to control editors below them in order to avoid retribution by their own bosses. Directors of television and radio were also regular participants in weekly meetings of central party committees. In this way top communist leaders were able to use the chain of authority to control the mass media directly. Such actions were particularly evident in the area of television.

These developments can be seen as a response to earlier party actions in the 1960s, when local and even central communist party institutions were often more supportive of relative press liberalization than state censors themselves. Many observers and participants in events at that time have argued that criticism of local affairs in the mass media beginning in the 1960s eventually led to wider critiques of the political order as a whole, helping to foster political reforms in 1968.[10] After the reestablishment of hard-line communist control in the early 1970s, many of those journalists responsible for the development of a critical press were forced to leave the profession and the country. Dogma came to characterize the post-1968 press. Finally, control over the media was reinforced through the power of the *nomenklatura* and its own practice of self-censorship. Editors-in-chief were required to be party members (with the possible exception of less important regional newspapers) and members of the communist party were given an advantage in employment within the mass media. The particular organizational affiliation of newspapers also made a difference. The communist daily *Pravda* provided higher salaries than other dailies, had the highest circulation (reinforced by lower subsidies for other dailies and compulsory subscriptions in some areas of the party and state) and enjoyed a higher level of technological infrastructure. Ironically, all these advantages were critical in ensuring that *Pravda* could survive the dramatic political changes in Czechoslovakia in 1989.

Given these forms of institutional control, it is not surprising that only with the rise of *glasnost* and *perestroika* in the Soviet Union did a new generation of journalists in Czechoslovakia attempt to publish articles that were in any way critical. However, even in these conditions journalists were initially cautious, covering topics which were only indirectly political, such as ecological problems. There were some signs of new ideas, primarily in periodicals established during the last years of communist rule that were outside the mainstream press (such as the cultural weekly *Literárny týždenník*). Yet conservative editors-in-chief of most of the important dailies, together with state television and radio, resisted such changes up to the Velvet (or as it is termed in Slovakia, the Gentle) Revolution itself.[11] Change was by no means incremental, as in the USSR or elsewhere. However, one source of information the Czechoslovak government could not control was the large degree to which foreign media reached the public, informing them of changes elsewhere in Eastern Europe.[12] In the end, it was by and large lower-level editors who forced their superiors to capitulate during the events of November 1989, and cover accurately the unfolding democratization process.

To summarize, the more restrictive political and media structures of Czechoslovakia in comparison with most Central and East European countries resulted in more radical, faster and deeper changes in the press in the first years after 1989. Yet this change did not necessarily lead to the pluralization and democratization of the press, particularly later with the formation of an independent Slovakia. During the period from 1989 to the summer of 1992, the Public Against Violence or PAV (the Slovak counterpart to the Czech Civic Forum) and its allies held sway in the Slovak parliament. With its eventual disintegration and the subsequent break-up of Czechoslovakia, the populist Movement for a Democratic Slovakia, or HZDS, built to a large degree on the charismatic personality of the machiavellian Vladimír Mečiar, came to dominate the politics of an independent Slovakia. HZDS domination of Slovak politics has continued almost unabated into the present; since its rise to power the government has clearly sought to establish control over the media, and has so far been quite successful, stunting the creation of independent media.

## Post-Communist Constitutional Provisions for the Freedom of the Press

After the overthrow of the communist regime in Czechoslovakia, the most important legal changes that affected the media could be found in the Constitution, the criminal and civil codes, and the law of the press. Modification of the criminal code abolished those paragraphs defining as criminal activity 'provocation' and 'subversion' by the press, film, radio and television broadcasting – both of which previously carried a minimum of one year and a maximum of five years' imprisonment. Criminal activity in what had been defined as 'press carelessness' was also abolished. However, two important paragraphs remained intact. These related to 'defamation' of either the state or its representatives. Although the category of state defamation has not been used since November 1989, probably owing to its legacy of abuse by the previous regime (although it should be noted that there were police investigations in this area, none leading to charges, however), personal defamation of state representatives has been utilized by the government on a number of occasions, with some success, to muzzle journalists who allegedly slander or criticize the leadership. While there have been legitimate issues of slander in some cases, in others it has been apparent that the government has been more interested in intimidating the press.

In other areas relating to freedom of speech, changes in the civil code have also strengthened personal rights, among which are included the right of privacy and the right of financial compensation for illegal interference in this area. The modification of the law of the press also allowed for the private publication of newspapers and magazines and also the participation of foreign capital in the print media. In January 1991 the Federal Assembly approved a so-called List of Basic Rights and Freedoms which is – as is the case with most Czechoslovak federal statutes – still a part of this present Slovak legal system. This statute, modelled on European variants, defined a broad range of personal rights, including rights related to freedom of expression and the right to information.

## Institutional Legacies, Political Transition and Media Structures

### State-Run Television and Radio

Despite the technical provisions for open communication and a free press, the level of state influence in the Slovak media is high, with variations depending on the form of mass communication. Television in post-communist Czechoslovakia initially consisted of three television channels*: a national channel, covering most of the country, a regional channel each for the Czech Republic and Slovakia, and a third channel, covering only about 20 per cent of the country, which had originally broadcast Soviet television. After the dissolution of Czechoslovakia these channels and their

---

* It should be noted that Slovak Television was eastablished as a legal entity in spring 1991. Until then there were two national channels only (except for the channel which broadcast Soviet television).

frequencies were divided between the two new states. While the Czech Republic moved towards the partial privatization of state television, similar moves in Slovakia were hindered by divergent political elites and political interest groups. Only one national Slovak television channel has so far been privately licensed, and this did not occur until 1995. The new channel began operations in late summer 1996.[13] As for the other two major channels, there are plans for the public Slovak Television to broadcast in future on one terrestrial and one satellite channel, while the second terrestrial channel will be privatized. Since early 1995 there has also existed one private television station on satellite and cable systems (see below).

In the area of radio broadcasting there exists a similar arrangement, with four state-run channels. There are a number of private radio stations, although these tend to be much shorter in range and lacking the kind of economic resources enjoyed by their state-owned counterparts. Yet state broadcasting has not been immune to economic constraints. As early as 1990 broadcasting institutions came under pressure to fire hundreds of employees, under the threat of a dramatic reduction in state subsidies. This in turn helped to increase support at both Slovak Television and Slovak Radio for greater independence from federal control. The federal government in Prague opposed this move, although there was support among the management of federal radio to establish independent Czech and Slovak radio stations. Regional governments also favoured the idea, seeing it as a way to gain greater power over broadcasting and the financial resources (such as user fees) which supported it.

While Slovak Television and Slovak Radio saw organizational independence as a way of gaining control over programming and over economic revenue, no clear consideration was given to how such changes would affect the long-term role of the electronic media in Slovakia as a public service institution. Media impartiality was not well defined, making television and radio prone to manipulation. For example, the first post-communist director of Slovak Television, Roman Kaliský, emphasized the need for impartiality in television broadcasts, but he also noted at the same time that Slovak Television was 'an important informational medium of the Slovak parliament and Slovak government' to serve the democratization of Slovak society.[14]

The first post-communist government of Slovakia (while still a part of Czechoslovakia, in 1990) did not pass any new legislation on public broadcasting institutions, although the new government promised to create public-service and news institutions that were more independent of the federal authorities. While the federal government declared its support in favour of media diversification, it also argued that it 'considered it necessary to keep control over state radio and television broadcasting, as it is an important democratic tool in realizing the information needs of the state and society and specific aspects of national culture'.[15] During 1990, this question of regional broadcasting institutions (either with or without a separate federal counterpart) became one of the central elements in discussions regarding the new constitutional arrangements of Czechoslovakia. The tension generated by these issues of regional versus federal power in the area of the media peaked in November 1990, when both state electronic broadcasting institutions in Slovakia declared their readiness to strike over this issue.

In May 1991, only two months after federal law gave such rights to the Slovak National Council, the Slovak parliament finally passed its own legislation regarding Slovak Television and Slovak Radio, under which both broadcasting institutions became 'public'. However, no legal documents ever clarified what in fact the term 'public' entails. To a large extent it appears that the parliament and government were reluctant to define this term, finding the ambiguity useful in serving their needs. Such ambiguity, for example, has made it relatively easy for parliament to amend the law on radio and television significantly on several occasions since 1991, notably in the area of supervisory boards for radio and television. The most important change in this area took place following parliamentary elections in 1992 and the rise of the HZDS to power. At that time the new parliament simplified the process by which members of the supervisory boards were elected in such a way that a simple majority in parliament could elect and dismiss their members. In other words, political influence by the parliament was firmly established over state-run television and radio, given their ability to control the supervisory boards and the power of the boards to propose to parliament the dismissal or election of the directors of both broadcasting institutions.

In short, the transition of state-owned broadcasting into a truly independent public service sector was successfully blocked, soon after the electronic media in Slovakia had gained some freedom from federal authority. These institutional changes have allowed the government quite easily to carry out changes in personnel (at the board, television and radio levels). This has been particularly evident since the most recent parliamentary election in November 1994, when the HZDS returned to power after the party had been out of power for several months.

*Private Electronic Broadcasting*

As mentioned above, the role of the private sector in the electronic media in Slovakia remains limited. The first private radio broadcasting began operations in Slovakia in June 1990, as a combination of French radio broadcasts and programmes by Slovak university students. This station was not officially licensed, but existed by taking advantage of gaps in legislation concerning the media – typical for all East European countries shortly after the collapse of communism. There were numerous applicants for private broadcasting licences, but Slovakia lacked institutions with effective jurisdiction in this area. These applications were initially handled at the national level through a special committee of the federal government; in May 1992 this power was transferred to the newly-established Council of the Slovak Republic for Radio and Television Broadcasting.

Private television has been much more restricted, although limited transmissions began in Slovakia as early as 1993 in the form of a regional channel, TV Sever (TV North). Since that time more than 20 private local cable television channels have emerged, although their national impact is obviously restricted by their links with local cable services. Many provide some limited news services, usually concentrated on local issues. Since 1995 there has been one national satellite cable channel, VTV, which does broadcast its own news, but the differences between its news programmes and those of state-run television are minor. Part of this may reflect the fact that VTV apparently has strong connections with the ruling HZDS.[16] This, combined with the audience restrictions created by broadcasting only via satellite and cable technologies, may explain why VTV had attracted only some ten per cent of the country's total viewing audience by the end of 1995. In fact, the greatest competition for Slovak Television is the Czech private television station Nova, even though its coverage of Slovakia is limited. The new private terrestrial station, Markíza, began broadcasting in late 1996; its impact on the media market as a whole thus remains unknown.

*The Print Media*

Within the print media, privatization and diversification have been much more evident, although the attempted pressure on them from the government and political parties have on some occasions been no less severe. At the time of the transition from communist rule in 1989 and early 1990 there were essentially three groups of newspapers. The first of these comprised the most prominent newspapers, including *Pravda*, the organ of the communist party, the trade union paper *Práca*, and *Smena*, the daily of the communist youth league. During the events of November–December 1989 *Pravda* had the highest circulation in Slovakia, standing at more than 400,000 copies. By the first half of 1990 this had dropped to around 380,000, and by June, when the new government limited its supply of paper, its circulation dropped to below 300,000. By 1992 *Pravda*'s circulation had fallen to around 240,000. Despite this decline in circulation, *Pravda* has remained one of the most influential publications, strongly critical of the new government and the process of economic reform, although it enjoyed a circulation of only some 165,000 copies in early 1995. The daily *Práca*, thanks to greater access to paper supplies, maintained a circulation of over 200,000 copies during the first years after 1989, although afterwards it saw an even sharper drop in circulation, to around 70,000 copies on weekdays in 1995, brought about in part by its increasing cover price, making it too expensive for many to purchase regularly. In 1992 its circulation stood at about 140,000.

*Práca* and *Smena* underwent a more rapid period of transition in both content and staff. During the first years after the fall of communism, *Práca* was noted for its publication of long extracts from Prime Minister Mečiar's regular weekly televised speeches and the often extremist statements of nationalist forces. *Smena*, which developed into a politically liberal publication, enjoyed a circulation of almost 130,000 copies at the beginning of 1990, but eventually, owing to rising costs and a personnel shake-up instigated by the government in the first days of 1993 while the paper was still under state ownership, its circulation declined to about 20–25,000 copies by 1995. Many of the paper's staff subsequently left to form their own daily, entitled *Sme*; after a period of stagnation, in 1995 *Smena* merged with *Sme* under the latter's name. *Pravda* holds about 13 per cent of Slovak readership, *Práca* eight per cent, and *Sme* six per cent. These numbers, however, pale in comparison to the front-runner, the daily tabloid *Nový Čas* ('New Time'), which commands some 27 per cent. It is significant that *Nový Čas* is not only the most popular paper, but one of only two dailies in which there is majority foreign ownership (in this case, an Austrian firm).[17] Also belonging to this group of publications are the pro-government *Slovenská republika*, with a circulation of around 70,000, and the daily sports paper *Šport Niké*, with 80,000 copies. While the daily *Národná obroda* ('National Reawakening') is, like most papers, struggling with low circulation (approximately 40,000 copies), it also belongs to this category. Both *Slovenská republika* and *Národná obroda* were funded directly or with the partial assistance of state institutions. This is also true regarding the new daily published since January 1996, *Nová smena mladých* ('New Shift of Youth' which collapsed after a few months).

A second group of publications is that of the less popular but still relatively influential dailies with circulations of between 35,000 and 70,000 copies. During the years 1990–92 a number of political dailies fell into this category, such as *Slovenský denník* ('Slovak Daily' published by the Christian Democratic Movement), *Verejnosť* ('Public') and *Telegraf*, both close to right-wing parties, and *Koridor*, close to the HZDS. All these dailies failed within their first few years of publication. Finally, there is a third group of publications with very low circulation, such as the regional daily *Hlas ludu* ('Voice of the People') and *Korzo* ('Promenade'), with a circulation of 30,000 copies or less.

While there has been a common tendency since 1989 among all Slovak political parties to establish their own daily newspapers or weekly periodicals throughout the post-communist period, for these and other publications one of the biggest obstacles has been the sheer lack of newsprint, the inadequate capacity of printing facilities and the limitations inherent in the state-owned distribution service – all legacies of the planned economy. There was also the lack of skilled journalists and, later on, the rising cover price of newspapers (which increased tenfold from 1989 to 1995, a result of increases in such inputs as newsprint, distribution costs and news agency fees) which could not be covered by advertising or subsidies. One observer has noted that 'in spite of such unfavourable conditions there has been a growth in the number of publications between 1989 and 1993 from 326 to 753 ... and in numbers of dailies from 12 to 20',[18] yet most of these magazines and journals have had a short life. Many of the new established daily papers also did not survive for long, although at the end of 1995 there were still 19 dailies.

In terms of privatization, the separation of newspapers from their state owners was a complicated and questionable process. The staff of the former communist party's *Pravda* reorganized themselves in 1990 as a joint-stock company, retaining the publication's left-wing orientation. However, in 1995 *Pravda*'s publisher was purchased by Harvar Investment, an investment group which apparently has ties with Mečiar. The labour newspaper *Práca* also was reorganized as a joint-stock company, although its ownership connections with the trade union remains in place. In the more tumultuous case of *Smena*, the paper was nationalized after 1989 and put under the control of a supervisory body chosen by (and largely submissive to) the government, leading to the subsequent political interference mentioned above. Although *Smena* merged into *Sme*, its main advertiser (a Slovak investment company), was temporarily placed until the control of the ministry of finance in 1995 on the basis of accusations of financial wrong-doing. Such actions raise questions concerning the long-term prospects for its journalistic independence.

At the local level, privatization has in some cases been equally complicated by city councillors. In October 1990 the evening daily newspaper in the city of Košice detached itself from the municipal council because of the high degree of interference in the paper by the local authorities. The council called the paper's editors a 'red mafia' and created a new paper to reassert control over the local press (though this new paper under council control eventually failed).

## Political Attitudes and Government Intervention

The relationship between government, state and media in post-communist

Slovakia has varied not only depending on the sector of the media, but also over time. While there were already tensions between the media and political leaders at the beginning of 1990, following the rise of the HZDS in 1992 the government has increasingly sought to stifle and control the media.

During the immediate period after the fall of communism from 1989 to 1992 the power elite which emerged in Slovakia was made up in large part of environmentalists, scientists, teachers, artists and actors, connected to the largely pro-reform and pro-federation Public Against Violence. While it might be imagined that their relationship with a newly liberalized media would have been a harmonious one, even during this early period the relationship between the two was commonly viewed as highly conflictual. The new political elite (particularly on the federal level) often accused journalists of displaying an excessively critical and anti-reformist stance, suggesting that the mass media were deliberately engaged in manipulating the inexperienced masses. After the break-up of PAV and the pro-reform elite's poor showing in the elections of 1992, they repeatedly blamed the mass media for their failure, raising the possibility of collusion between the media, representatives of the 'second power elite' – the HZDS, which emerged out of the nationalist and pro-Mečiar wing of PAV – and members of the former secret police.[19]

These speculations seem only partially correct. More important in explaining media behaviour during this time is the fact that like most Slovaks, journalists lacked a real understanding of democratic politics or market economics, and were sharply divided on the issue of constitutional rearrangement. The policies of more populist and demagogic political leaders have simply been easier to follow for the mass media as a whole. The media's criticism of the first set of democratic leaders in Slovakia, as well as of economic reform and the Czechoslovak federation, found a favourable response among most members of Slovak society, and were thus echoed by much of the media – not dissimilar to their pre-1989 role.

This ambiguous relationship between the state, the government and the media has resulted in a great degree of political interference in the latter, particularly television broadcasting. As noted earlier, changes in media personnel (and consequent changes in the political content of programmes, especially the news) have been effected by a number of different methods, both direct and indirect. For example, that television is a major centre of power struggles in Slovakia is attested to by the fact that in the six years since the collapse of communism there have been eight directors of Slovak national television. In contrast, the director of Slovak Radio was able to hold his post until the end of 1994, when he was dismissed soon after the first session of the newly-elected parliament.

Government influence in the print sector has been a more complicated affair. One basic problem is that since 1989 there has been a proliferation of publications under various forms of private ownership, including those controlled by various political parties. A second obstacle is the relative impracticality of reintroducing state censorship. New ways of pressure thus had to be found, and a number of attempts to limit the freedom of the press were made, with mixed results. In this process, two basic factors have framed the struggle over the mass media from 1989 to 1996:

(a)  The general belief of post-communist elites that the electronic media have a critical role to play in creating a 'correct' view of reality through the shaping of public opinion; and

(b)  An insufficient de-étatisation of electronic mass media.[20]

This is particularly ironic, given the fact that it was Slovakia in 1991 that adopted the first laws in Eastern Europe on 'public broadcasting institutions', changes which should technically have created media that were more independent.

Even shortly after 1989, both the Czechoslovak president and the prime minister already began to express their disapproval of the media, criticizing their actions and their content; such complaints were to become a permanent feature in attitudes of post-communist politicians towards the media in Czechoslovakia and in its successor states. Initially, however, these complaints were seen as constructive, related to the belief that the media paid too little attention to the work and statements of governmental institutions. Later, however, such arguments were used to justify governmental support for specific daily newspapers and other publications which supported the ruling party.

Methods used by the state in its policy of pressure upon the mass media during the transition period varied, but typically fell into one of several categories, with some obvious overlap: economic instruments, arguments based on supposed 'ethical' standards, legal and technical mechanisms, purges and patronage.

*Economic Instruments*

In the 1995 state budget, proposed amendments threatened a new set of legal encroachments on press freedom, combining economic and legal instruments. Particularly important was the suggestion that the ministry of culture would be empowered to designate certain publications as 'non-commercial', and subject them to a lower rate of taxation. What criteria the ministry would use in such a determination was not defined, casting further suspicions on the proposal. By contrast, media outlets with a significant amount of foreign capital would be taxed at a rate three to five times higher than those domestically owned. While this legislation was not passed, the proposal was a clear sign that media independence could not be taken for granted.

Another form of economic pressure was the use of indirect government subsidies, which were denied to publications that were seen as over-critical of the government. One example of this occurred in Slovakia in 1991, when Prime Minister Ján Čarnogurský refused a request for financial support from the editor-in-chief of the liberal weekly *Kultúrny život*. This refusal was directly linked to the weekly's recent publication of an article which was seen by Čarnogurský as hostile to Christian beliefs. Such practices have become common in Slovakia since independence, with indirect state subsides given disproportionately to papers seen as government supporters (such as the HZDS-owned *Slovenská Republika*), while liberal publications have been cut off.

Monetary pressure was also used against the electronic media. In 1993, the government refused to allocate money from the approved state budget for Slovak Radio and Slovak Television, with the aim of forcing the institution to revise the content of its broadcasts and fire some journalists. Throughout the transition from communism, the financial dependence of the electronic media on state support has been one of the main obstacles to editorial independence. This was compounded by the limitations of a small market (limiting the potential of advertising income) and the reluctance of parliament to pass laws enacting and enforcing compulsory fees that would secure a regular income for state television and radio (although such a law was eventually passed in 1995).

Under such pressure, changes in the content and staffing in the electronic media have been evident. In 1993 major editorial changes in many sectors of the news (such as at *Rádiožurnál*, the most popular radio news programme in Slovakia) were widely viewed as a bargain struck to retain state economic support by shifting to a more pro-government orientation. Given that such programmes have an important impact on shaping the political attitudes of the Slovak public, the implications are broad and serious.

*Ethical Arguments*

Parliament has also turned towards ethical arguments on several occasions – something not easily defined and open to interpretation and misuse. One of the clearest example was in the above-mentioned case of *Kultúrny život* and the government's refusal to provide subsidies to the publication in 1991. With the establishment of Slovakia as an independent state, the use of such arguments has intensified. Beginning in 1992 the government began regularly to criticize journalists' work as 'unethical', which can be translated as 'critical of the government'. This was best captured in Prime Minister Mečiar's comment that journalists should practise 'ethical self-regulation'. What the prime minister meant was clearly a form of self-censorship and not ethical reporting; it was in fact Mečiar who in 1995 presented awards to *Slovenská Republika* and the anti-Semitic *Zmena*, two of the least ethical but pro-government periodicals in Slovakia.[21]

Recently, parliament has sought to turn these vague ethical arguments into law. In 1995 draft legislation submitted by coalition members proposed a so-called 'Declaration on Ethics in Journalism' which would delimit the scope of 'proper' journalistic activity. In response, one judge of the of Constitutional Court of the Slovak Republic criticized the proposal as nonsensical:

> Control over public opinion expresses itself through ethical norms. If state authorities create norms for the public instead of the public themselves, it turns the relationship between the two on its head. In this way the state decides the content and scope of ethical norms through which citizens influence public authority, and in doing so it predetermines the method, condition and scope of control for the state itself.[22]

The question of former collaborators and agents of the State Security and Intelligence Service, or ŠtB, has also become a source of conflict and state power during the period 1990–92. At the beginning of 1992 almost 3,000 Slovak journalists (and approximately the same number of Czech journalists) underwent a process of 'lustration' on the initiative of the State Intelligence Service. These lists were given to both national prime ministers, and shortly thereafter they appeared in right-wing dailies in each republic. This was in keeping with arguments by those in power that, at a minimum, journalists had been individually blackmailed by former members of the secret police to discredit the government, or worse, that there existed a widespread conspiracy between journalists and former agents to overthrow the democratic government. This conspiracy argument continued to prevail within the following government, and was later expanded to include foreign powers as well. Prime Minister Mečiar in 1993 raised the possibility that at least 40 prominent journalists were being paid by forces abroad to write against the government.

*Legal Mechanisms*

The creation and transformation of legislative bodies in Czechoslovakia and its successor states has had a direct influence on the development of media laws and related statutes in Slovakia. As early as 1990–91 the Czechoslovak Federal Assembly ceded much of its powers in the area of the media to the two national parliaments, and this gave the Slovak legislative institutions the power to influence the course of media change even before the dissolution of Czechoslovakia. Yet in early 1991 Ján Čarnogurský threatened to veto any legislation on private radio and television for a minimum of two years, effectively blocking privatization. It should be noted that this was done through pressure by the managements of both institutions. Also, in regard to public television broadcasting Čarnogurský argued that 'if the Slovak Republic were to be responsible for financing its public television, it should have the right to regulate it as well'.[23] While these arguments may seem to reflect primarily the struggle over federal broadcasting, they are also indicative of the attitudes of the first power elite towards the media at that time.

As an eventual compromise, resulting from both domestic pressure and international advice, Slovakia and the Czech Republic passed legislation on public broadcasting in early 1991. Development of the dual media plan in Slovakia, however, remained limited by legal barriers, and this remained unchanged with Slovakia's independence. In the spring of 1994 the Slovak parliament twice refused to approve licences for private television broadcasting, despite the change in government between the two proposals.

*Technical Mechanisms*

Technical mechanisms have been used primarily to stifle information from abroad. The best example was against Radio Free Europe (RFE) Slovak broadcasts on medium wave (AM wavelength). After repeated criticism of RFE, in December 1993 the Slovak minister of communication and telecommunications gave notice that a new treaty for the further broadcasting of RFE would not be possible. Officially, the explanation given was that such broadcast frequencies were necessary for future Slovak Radio broadcasts. This justification, however, contradicted the statements of the superintendent of Slovak Radio, who repeatedly denied that his organization had asked for these frequencies. After negotiations between both sides, the Slovak ministry reluctantly agreed to extend RFE's broadcast rights. RFE transmissions still faced interference; in March 1994, during a period of serious conflict between parliament and Prime Minister Mečiar, these transmissions were ordered by the ministry to be stopped for a few hours.

Further criticism of RFE arose during the summer of 1995. Consequently, while in mid-1995 the Board for Radio and Television Broadcasting did issue a licence for further broadcasting by RFE, this licence was only temporary, set to expire at the end of 1996. The board justified this action by labelling the broadcasts of RFE as biased against the government.[24]

*Personal Purges*

As mentioned above, there have been substantial changes in the leadership of the media in Slovakia. In Slovak television, eight superintendents and five senior editors of the main news programmes have been dismissed in the past six years. At Slovak Radio, two directors and at least three editors-in-chief of news programmes have been dismissed as well. In the print media such actions have been more limited given the lack of direct state control. However, one case which stands out, and has already been mentioned in passing, is the firing of the editor-in-chief of the daily *Smena*, Karol Ježík. *Smena* had remained under state ownership since 1989 and was noted for its critical attitude toward Mečiar; in the first days of Slovak independence in 1993 Ježík was fired by the paper's managing board, which cited business reasons by way of explanation. It was widely understood, however, that Ježík's dismissal had been instigated by Mečiar.[25] Since 1995, the increasingly close links between media owners and political elites raise the danger that such actions may become more common at other papers in the future.

*Patronage*

It is not accidental that many within the media have become members of the political elite themselves. One of the best examples is that of the former senior editor of the popular news programme *Rádiožurnál*, Ivan Mjartan. Criticized repeatedly for this pro-HZDS bias, which he denied, shortly before the 1992 parliamentary elections it was discovered that he was on the list of parliamentary candidates for the HZDS (which had been kept secret); after this was revealed Mjartan disavowed that he had any desire for a seat in parliament. As a result of pressure from within the staff of *Rádiožurnál* he eventually left his post, later winning a parliamentary seat that he had publicly denied any interest in. Shortly thereafter he was appointed by the new government to be the first Slovak ambassador to the Czech Republic. Other journalists have clearly aligned themselves with the HZDS, becoming members of parliament or, as in the case of two journalists from *Rádiožurnál*, staff members to the cabinet. This overlap between state functions and media functions has in some instances become extreme, and is not limited to the state-run media. For example, one of the editors of the pro-governmental daily *Slovenská Republika* simultaneously acts as the official spokesman of Slovak Intelligence. Members of the pro-government Association of Slovak Journalists have similarly risen to high-ranking positions within the ministry of culture and Slovak Television, while others have been given positions on the supervisory boards of radio and television broadcasting.

Finally, as noted above, patronage also has taken the form of governmental prizes and awards. In 1995 the government awarded prizes in journalism on the basis of nominations by the pro-government Association of Slovak Journalists; alongside the pro-government *Slovenská Republika* and *Zmena*, individual recipients included two HZDS members of parliament.

## Media Democratization, External Models, and the Future

This relationship between the media and political forces in Slovakia indicates clearly that impartiality and press independence as enshrined in the West has not been taken to heart. This is so despite the efforts of individuals both inside and outside the country who have sought to restructure the media on the basis of external models. Since 1989, the strongest theoretical influences on Czechoslovak and Slovak media institutions have come from the United States, in particular, the American norms of press media; American institutions in particular have been strongly involved in developing a free press in Central and Eastern Europe. Most books, textbooks and journals dealing with journalism and mass communications which are available in Slovakia come from American sources as well. However, in reality the impact of American models and ideas on the Slovak media has been limited; such concepts and practices remain quite different from West European experiences, which are themselves closer to the East European tradition. American specialists appear to miss these differences.

By way of example, a group of experts from the Annenberg Program in Washington invited to Czechoslovakia in November 1990 proposed to the Czechoslovak federal government a number of policies for media reform, which included the following recommendations: that much of the regulatory power over the mass media should remain in federal hands, such as in the area of transmission frequencies; that Czechoslovakia should avoid the 'Belgian' approach of three different television networks run by three different bureaucracies; that the government should establish an independent commission which would decide questions of licensing; that public broadcasting institutions should be insulated from the federal and national governments; that the political influence of the presidency and parliament in the media should be minimized; and that diversity should be encouraged by a greater role for independent production.[26]

In retrospect these proposals are quite informative. Most important among them is the idea to establish an independent supervisory body and the concept of a centralized structure for television. The notion of establishing independent supervisory boards did in fact work in Slovakia until the summer of 1992 when the new government effectively eliminated their autonomy. However, the argument of avoiding the 'Belgian approach' proved impossible owing to the pressures to establish an equal partnership between the two republics, where media institutions themselves played a key role as a critical tool in this struggle. Centralization would only have further exacerbated these tensions.

As for more general Western concepts concerning the role of the media, these again have been primarily American, classical liberal arguments. A translated handbook for journalists, provided by the Washington-based World Press Freedom Committee, has been freely distributed among journalists in Slovakia and throughout Central and Eastern Europe.[27] In such publications the main task of journalists is defined as performing a watch-dog role and as a conduit of information for citizens in order to enable them to vote intelligently or to exert pressure on the government.[28]

These expected roles of journalists and journalism in European countries – Central European and elsewhere – are complicated by what the Canadian professor of journalism George Frajkor defines as 'the status of the European journalist ... as an intellectual leader of society, whose mission is to influence events. The American reporter is presumed to be an investigator of events and a recorder of them.'

There is also at least one other factor that separates European legacies from those in America. As Frajkor asserts, Europe's statist tradition means that the level of government involvement in the media remains much higher than what is acceptable in the US.[29] This is consistent with the present discussion among West European media experts on the impact of business pressures on a free press and the question of 'positive' versus 'negative' freedoms in communication.

Furthermore, in Eastern Europe discussion centres on the need for governments to use the mass media as an element of unification during the complicated and painful process of transition from socialist society to a liberal-democratic and market-based system. In the case of Slovakia this kind of interest in the mass media has been further complicated by the creation of a new and independent state out of Czechoslovak federal system, thus strengthening this idea of the media as a state instrument for national unity.

In conclusion, the diversification of information sources in Slovakia has been significantly hindered by objective and subjective conditions. This has contributed to the political polarization of society. Media that are too partisan, whether private or state-owned, are clearly not the best method to serve the creation of civil society. However, the process of transition in Slovakia is not yet finished; there is the possibility that the emerging private sector, particularly in the area of the electronic media, will undermine governmental control over broadcast institutions. Together with the pressure from an impartial press, there is the chance that a more independent set of public service institutions will develop. For now, though, governmental influence seems unlikely to vanish.

## NOTES

1. See Jozef Borísek, 'Straníckosť a sloboda tlače v socialistickej spoločnosti', in *Otázky žurnalistiky*, Vol.21, No.2 (1978), p.4; Juraj Vojtek, *V.I.Lenin a tisk nového typu* (Praha: Vydavatelství a nakladatelství Novinář, 1986) p.7.
2. See Edward Taborsky, *Communism in Czechoslovakia, 1948–1960* (Princeton, NJ: Princeton University Press, 1961).
3. Frank L. Kaplan, *Winter Into Spring: The Czechoslovak Press and the Reform Movement, 1963–1968* (Boulder, CO: East European Monographs, 1977) p.22.
4. The precise data chronicling this decline vary. For instance Dušan Tomášek writes that there was a decline from 37 dailies in 1947 to 11 in 1953. Kaplan notes a decline from 18 dailies (although from what initial date is unclear) to 11 by 1952, with altogether 350 publications suppressed during that period. Taborsky offers an interesting comparison from the pre-communist era: by 1958 there were only 17 dailies in the whole of Czechoslovakia, whereas in 1940 there were some 55 published in the Czech provinces alone. It should also be noted, however, that following this decline there was again a slow increase in the number of dailies published from 1953 onwards. This reflected an increased feeling of security with the firm establishment of censorship mechanisms, and thus a modest expansion of the press was no longer considered a direct threat. See Dušan Tomášek, *Pozor cenzurováno! aneb zo Života soudružíky cenzury* (Praha: Vydavatelství a nakladatelství MV ČR 1994), p.8; Kaplan, *Winter into Spring*, p.18; and Taborsky, *Communism in Czechoslovakia*, p.560.
5. Tomášek, *Pozor cenzurováno!*, p.8.
6. See George Schöpflin, *Censorship and Political Communication in Eastern Europe: A Collection of Documents* (London: Pinter, 1977), p.14; Kaplan, *Winter into Spring*, p.79; and Luboš Šefčák, 'O poslednej novelizácii tlačového zakona', *Otázky žurnalistiky*, Vol.33, No.1 (1991), p.16.
7. Tomášek, *Pozor cenzurováno!* p.78.
8. Dušan Hamšík, *Writers Against Rulers* (London: Hutchinson, 1971), p.18.
9. Jiři Hochman, 'Words and Tanks: The Revival, The Struggle, The Agony and Defeat (1968–1968)', in Jiři Pehe (ed.), *The Prague Spring: A Mixed Legacy* (Washington, DC: Freedom House, 1988), p.27.
10. Juraj Fabian, 'O zložitej ceste k slobode tlače', interview in *Praca*, 8 Jan. 1991, pp.1–3.
11. With perhaps one exception: the daily newspaper *Smena*.
12. The number of listeners to Western radio stations in Czechoslovakia increased dramatically during the last year of communism. Thus, from 1982 to 1989 the Voice of America saw an increase of its audience from 20 to 32 per cent, Radio Free Europe from 16 to 29 per cent, and the BBC from 10 to 15 per cent: Oskar Krejčí, 'Prečo to prasklo', *Pravda na nedelu*, 25 Jan. 1991, p.5.
13. Shortly before elections in 1992 two companies were awarded a licence to operate the third channel jointly, although they were unable to reach an agreement.
14. Eva Vrbicka, 'Česta spat nemožna', *Práca*, 31 March 1990, p.6.
15. 'Programové vyhlásenie vlady 'ČSFR', *Práca*, 4 July 1990, p.3.
16. Sharon Fisher, 'Slovak Media Under Pressure', *Transition*, 6 Oct. 1995, pp.7–9.
17. For further details see Andrej Školkay, 'Slovak Broadcasting Tightens its Grip on the Airwaves', *Transition* Vol.2, No.8 (19 April 1996), pp.18–21.
18. Vladimír Holina, 'Zmeny v masových médiách na Slovensku', *Parlamentný kuriér*, No.2 (1994), pp.29–30.
19. Ivo Grycz, 'Česko-Slovensko očami porazených', *Slobodný piatok*, 1994, No.44, p.9; Ladislav Snopko, 'Slovensko medzi baranom a baránkom', *Slovenské listy*, 1995, No.5, p.17.
20. Peter Schutz, 'Kde leží pieda slovenskej Darmovízie', *Domino efekt*, 1995, No.6, p.2.
21. Fisher, 'Slovak Media Under Pressure', p.9.
22. Jan Drgonec, 'Čas slobody prejavu v plienkach', *KMIT*, 1995, No.5, p.19.
23. David Webster, *Building Democracy: New Broadcasting Laws in East and Central Europe* (Washington, DC: Annenberg Washington Programme, 1992), p.10.
24. For details see Owen Johnson, 'Whose Voice? Freedom of Speech and the Media in Central Europe', in Al Hester and Kristina White (eds.), *Creating a Free Press in Eastern Europe*

(Athens, GA: The James M. Cox, Jr. Center for International Mass Communication Training and Research, 1991), pp.25–6.
25. Ibid., pp.34–5.
26. Webster, *Building Democracy*, p.14.
27. Malcolm F. Mallette (ed.), *Přírućka pro novináře střední a východní Evropy* (Washington, DC: World Press Freedom Committee, 1995).
28. Ibid., pp.44, 74–5.
29. George Frajkor, <gfrajkor@ccs.carleton.ca>, 'REPLY: Russian Media Theory: Does it Exist?', in EEMEDIA <eemedia@mcfeeley.cc.utexas.edu>, 4 Sept. 1995.

# Pluralization and the Politics of Media Change in Hungary

ANDRÁS LÁNCZI AND PATRICK H. O'NEIL

In Hungary, under the relatively benign rule of János Kádár's 'goulash communism', the media were less rigidly controlled than elsewhere in Eastern and Central Europe, permitting broader scope for debate. This affected the transition, in which some media spontaneously privatized themselves, with the involvement of foreign media conglomerates. By 1994, however, the government regained control over several important publications and otherwise fostered a more conservative press. The electronic media meanwhile remained overwhelmingly in state hands, and open conflict flared in 1992. The media became the focus of political battles, involving parliament, government, the constitutional court and the president, and purges of journalists and officials in the media led to assertions that little had changed since the communist regime. The question is whether control of the media will remain a spoil of election victory, or new legislation will establish a non-partisan framework for the future.

With the collapse of socialism in Eastern Europe one of the major struggles which has emerged is that between new political and economic relations and the legacies of state power. Under the old order, these spheres of power were merged into a single ruling entity, a party-state whose prime function was not simply to rule, but also to prevent the emergence of civil opposition at any level. Yet in the move to democracy, civil society and a free market, the disentanglement of these spheres of power has shown to be no easy task. The creation of independent loci of influence and rights – the dispersal of concentrated power – is difficult not only in practical terms, but also in the temptations that such powers create for political actors in the post-communist era. The old tools of hegemony can be utilized in the pursuit of the 'good', however that is defined by new political elites – the purging of state institutions, the elimination of rivals, the reinforcement of certain values at the expense of others, for instance.

While numerous institutional remnants of the old order can be seen in these terms, one that has attracted particular attention in this regard has been the press and broadcast media (from here on the term 'media' alone will be

András Lánczi is a professor in the Department of Political Science at the Budapest University of Economics; Patrick H. O'Neil is an assistant professor in the Department of Politics and Government at the University of Puget Sound, Tacoma, Washington.

used to refer to both the press and broadcast media). Newspapers, magazines, radio and television served as the central information and propaganda organs of the party-state, controlling and attempting to mould information in such a manner as to reinforce political control. But the end of communist rule did not mean the dissolution of media institutions themselves; these structures remained intact, part and parcel of the state order. Issues of privatization, of censorship and of bias inevitably became sources of bitter dispute as conflicting elites battled over the media as a source of civil society or a source of new political power.

These issues are generic to Eastern Europe, and former socialist states in general. Yet since the fall of communism in Eastern Europe we have seen that the paths taken down the road of media transformation have been markedly different from one state to the next. To a certain extent this can be attributed to the particular coalitions of power from state to state, but such developments are not merely the product of rational choice. Rather, it is the argument of this article that the trajectory of media change (or the lack of it) in Eastern Europe is to a large extent guided by institutional legacies carried over from the old order.

The role of the press in each East European case can be seen as illustrative of a larger institutional matrix, which differed from place to place. These unique institutional orders in turn shaped the manner of their own collapse, as well as the way in which the media 'transited' to the post-communist period. The manner of the transition thus created different institutional contexts, or legacies, under post-communism, which influenced the possibilities for and probabilities of certain kinds of change in the media. In short, the nature of the struggle over the media across Eastern Europe can be viewed as a function of its role under the previous order. The Hungarian case will serve as an illustration of this argument.

## 'Goulash Communism', the Hungarian Media and the Transition to Democracy

As a generalization, socialism as practised in Hungary from the 1960s onwards was known for its high degree of reformist pragmatism and the relative liberties given to the population. 'Goulash communism', as some termed it, was a product of the disastrous events of 1956, where one of the most repressive Stalinist regimes in Eastern Europe was overthrown and a revolution was put down only through the force of Soviet arms. Confronted with the option of using repression as a fundamental policy to maintain order, the new party secretary, János Kádár, chose instead to re-institutionalize the party-state on the basis of reform and the de-ideologization of the social sphere.

Kádár's policy, summarized in his oft-cited quotation that 'those who are not against us are with us', withdrew overt communist dogma, and replaced it with reformist economic policies and greater tolerance for social pluralism. The basic organizational tenets of socialist rule remained intact; indeed, in keeping with Philip Selznick's explanation of institutionalization (see the introductory article, above), beyond the organizational blueprints of the party-state, routines and policies were created to keep these structures intact.

By the late 1960s, Hungary, which only a decade earlier was the source of violent upheaval and repression, had developed into a model of tolerance and reform within the socialist camp. Alongside the so-called 'first' official society, a 'second' society of informal and tolerated practices had developed, embracing new institutional patterns meant to co-opt and pacify the population. Social dissent was channelled into this second society, which served as a pressure valve intended to mute opposition and enervate its power.

One of the major pillars of this institutional structure was the media. Elsewhere in Eastern Europe, rigid controls over the press prevented social influence in media content; social communication largely fragmented, to be replaced by an underground *samizdat* press (as in Poland), or, where this was not possible, by a network of rumour (as in Romania). While these also existed in Hungary, the official media themselves developed into a central institution for political debate, allowing for the semi-open discussion of sensitive topics precisely in order to dissipate the effects of such ideas. From the early 1970s onwards numerous intellectual and regional journals had appeared, among them *Tiszatáj*, *Új Írás*, *Jelenkor* and *Valóság*, which broadened the scope of debate. This was mirrored in the broadcast media, where programmes such as *168 Óra* and *Pánorama* covered sensitive topics and interviewed figures known to be critical of the party. Formal censorship on the part of the state was replaced by self-censorship, allowing for fluid lines of debate (and occasional sanction for stepping too far). As the Hungarian sociologist Elemér Hankiss described it, within the media the first and second society met and interacted:

> In a strange way, the second public sphere invaded the first. People, trespassing on the grounds of the first public sphere and symbolically expanding their freedom, openly discussed important issues, criticized the regime and attacked sacrosanct taboos; but they did all this in an allegorical and allusive language, the use and understanding of which became a societal game and a highly refined art. Everybody took part in this nation-wide connivance, the members of the ruling elite included. They swooped down only when allusions became too abusive or touched upon spots that were too sensitive.[1]

But by the late 1980s the means by which the party had maintained its social support began to turn into its greatest enemy. As changes within Soviet politics became more evident, the ruling Hungarian Socialist Workers' Party (*Magyar Szocialista Munkáspárt* – MSZMP) found itself at a loss how to respond. It had predicated its rule on the argument that it created a more tolerant form of dictatorship for its subjects in comparison with the rest of the bloc; now developments were making that justification obsolete. As the party stagnated and split into factions, unable to react to events, sectors of society began to press the second society into the first, incrementally expanding the political space for debate within Hungary.

This was to have a devastating effect on party power. The institutional order had already created the means by which social dissent could be expressed, if only in a limited manner; with the paralysis of the communist party, party-state institutions began to develop civic qualities of their own accord. The already semi-open media began to pluralize themselves at a dizzying pace, as new papers and journals appeared virtually overnight and as remaining official taboos were cast aside. Even central party and government newspapers soon became identified with party factions, using their readership to publicize their own views on political reform.

The transition in Hungary, compared to elsewhere in the region, was thus a process of political erosion rather than sudden failure. This is a critical point to understanding later developments. Unlike other, more rigid regimes, the reformist institutionalization upon which the party had based its security eventually created the opportunity and the vehicle by which civil society could penetrate and dismantle the party-state. This slow process of transition in turn had several important effects. First, the party elite was unable to dictate the terms of the transition, or create new institutional structures in an attempt to recast its rule (as in Romania, Bulgaria, or to a lesser extent Poland). While the MSZMP attempted to reorganize existing constitutional provisions in a last-ditch attempt to regroup party power more clearly within the state (through such devices as electoral laws and a strong presidency), these efforts ultimately failed, blocked by growing external opposition and internal fragmentation. They did, however, leave behind important institutional fragments, or what Adam Przeworski has called 'traces of extrication', that would have important effects later.

Second, given this slow erosion of party power, the political opposition which sprang up in 1987–88 did not need to combine into a mass-based 'front' movement as elsewhere, forming instead well-articulated political organizations in competition as much with one another as with the state (compared with such movements as Poland's Solidarity or Czechoslovakia's Civic Forum). No single political movement came to the fore in 1989 possessing a mandate to reshape the institutional landscape for good or ill.

This political fragmentation therefore meant that many crucial political reforms – such as those in the media – were to be obstructed by the dispersal of parliamentary power.

Third, in distinction from other East European countries, in Hungary the process of reform since the 1960s, and the role of the media in the increase in public voice since the late 1980s, meant that the post-communist media were able to carry over a certain degree of popular legitimacy. This denied the subsequent conservative government a popular mandate for radical reform, even though, for all intents and purposes, the media remained in the hands of journalists and managers who had laboured under the old regime.

A fourth point relates to the time-frame of the transition. As we noted above, in the end the MSZMP failed in its attempt to re-engineer its rule; by October 1989 radicals within the MSZMP at an extraordinary congress dissolved the party and formed a new Hungarian Socialist Party (MSZP) in an attempt to preserve some semblance of legitimacy in the face of rapid decline. The long period of the transition process did have an important effect, in that it gave many party and state organizations the chance to 'jump ship' prior to open elections in the spring of 1990.

## The Transformation of the Press

This last factor was particularly evident within the press. During the course of early 1990, as the end of communist power became evident, a number of state and party newspapers began to privatize themselves spontaneously, seeking to become independent organizations before a new government came to power. The largest national paper in terms of circulation, the party central daily *Népszabadság* divorced itself from the MSZP, selling a 40 per cent stake in the paper to the German conglomerate Bertelsmann AG. The government newspaper *Magyar Hírlap* similarly transformed itself into an independent business concern, which in turn sold a 40 per cent share of the paper to Robert Maxwell's Mirror Holding Company. The official newspaper of the trade unions, *Népszava*, also detached itself from state and labour connections, though without the help of foreign capital.

In what was perhaps the most publicized event, in early April 1990 seven county papers, formerly regional organs of the MSZMP, spontaneously privatized themselves, transferring full ownership to the German press magnate Axel Springer. Springer effectively paid nothing for these papers, other than to guarantee their maintenance. Ironically, then, the Hungarian press became the most highly privatized press in Eastern Europe, and also that with the greatest amount of foreign capital invested in it, while still under socialist rule, *before* free elections even took place.[2]

In the spring of 1990 the first open elections in Hungary since the late

1940s brought to power a conservative coalition government, composed of the dominant populist Hungarian Democratic Forum (*Magyar Demokrata Fórum* – MDF) alongside its two allies, the Smallholders' Party and the Christian Democrats. The MSZP, along with the liberal Free Democrats (*Szabad Demokraták Szövetsége* – SZDSZ) and the Young Democrats (*Fiatal Demokraták Szövetsége* – FIDESZ), formed the opposition. The head of the MDF, József Antall, became prime minister. Liberal and conservative hostilities, already intensified during the elections over the issue of which side hated communism more, quickly developed into parliamentary acrimony and deadlock.

In these new parliamentary struggles the press played an important role. Staffed by journalists from the socialist era, unaccustomed to standards as practised in Western democracies, much of what was printed consisted more of opinion than news, and, not surprisingly, much of this opinion was against the new conservative government. Thus, in the eyes of the new government, the press, now beyond the reach of the state to reorganize or privatize as it saw fit, remained in the hands of the old regime, staffed by former communists or liberal sympathizers whose enmity towards the new government was clear.[3] The MDF and its allies thus sought to use state power to create their own 'counter-hegemony' against the independent press.

This process unfolded in several steps. First, some remaining assets were privatized on the basis of ideological criteria. One example was the case of *Magyar Nemzet*, the only major daily which had not privatized itself prior to parliamentary elections. In 1990 the government blocked the attempt by the editorial staff to sell the paper to the Swedish daily *Dagens Nyheter*. The paper was subsequently sold to the French press concern Hersant, which was apparently viewed by the government as more ideologically conservative. Several months later many of the paper's journalists struck against the new editor, decrying the dismissal of several journalists in what they viewed as an attempt to steer the paper in a pro-government direction.[4]

Second, some press assets remained in state hands, and were reorganized into government publications. In 1990 the political weekly *Heti Magyarország* saw its editor fired over the protests of its staff and replaced by a government appointment. The publication subsequently turned in a strongly pro-government direction.[5]

Third, these assets were augmented by the creation of new mass publications which, although not directly state-owned, would back the ruling coalition. In early 1991 a new daily publication, entitled *Új Magyarország*, appeared on the stands, with an obvious pro-government and anti-opposition slant. While the paper was not technically state-owned, the corporation which owned it turned out to be a joint-stock company made of up shareholders who were largely state-owned firms.[6] The independent publication *Reggeli Pesti Hírlap*, which suffered severe losses following its inception in 1990, was also purchased by a pro-government foundation backed by state-owned industries and banks, renamed (to *Pesti Hírlap*) and transformed into a conservative ally of the government.[7]

While these actions clearly reflect the government's frustration at how the state press structure had 'escaped into the market' during the political transition, in fact these same market forces were to provide new opportunities for the government to increase its influence in the press. Although since 1990 some had raised fears over the excessive role of foreign capital in the Hungarian press market, one thing that was not expected was the rapidity with which much of this capital would be withdrawn.

The first major shift in the Hungarian press market was initiated by the death of Robert Maxwell in 1991, and the subsequent liquidation of his holdings. The government used this opportunity to repurchase shares in several papers which had been privatized by the former socialist government. *Esti Hírlap* and *Pest Megyei Hírlap* returned to the state fold; in the case of the latter, it was in turn sold to a private investor close to the Christian Democrats. One major daily which the government did not purchase, however, was Maxwell's *Magyar Hírlap*; it has been suggested that the price was simply too high for the government to purchase and avoid a public outcry (the paper was eventually sold to the Swiss Jürg Marquard Group).[8] The daily *Mai Nap* and the weekly *Reform*, purchased by Rupert Murdoch in 1990, were also resold to the state. By early 1994, even *Magyar Nemzet* had returned to state hands, after Hersant put the money-losing paper up for sale and found no private buyers.

Thus by 1994 the government had been able to create or gain control over a number of important daily and weekly publications, and had assisted in the development of a conservative press whose ownership links to the state were more attenuated. The government even assisted in the formation of a new journalist organization, the Community of Hungarian Journalists, to counter the Federation of Hungarian Journalists, a hold-over from the communist period.[9] In these efforts the government was loudly condemned by the domestic opposition and some foreign observers, who argued that a government-directed press had no role in an emerging democracy.[10]

However, even in the most optimistic estimates, it is clear that the government's steps to increase its influence in the press led to modest successes at best. For example, in 1993 the two daily newspapers considered closest to the government, *Új Magyarország* and *Pesti Hírlap*, had a combined readership share of about 160,000, compared with over one million for the socialist daily *Népszabadság*.[11] Here the government confronted the legacy of 'soft communism' under Kádár. As mentioned above, under that system the routines of reform and relative openness meant that the party and government dailies had been able to build up a large degree of popular legitimacy, which they were able to carry over into the post-socialist era. The government for all its efforts was unable to create a viable challenger to the existing dominant publications.

## The Battle for the Broadcast Media

The MDF-led coalition drew these same conclusions itself. As early as 1991 Imre Kónya, the head of the MDF's parliamentary faction, had argued in an internal report that the party was unlikely to increase its access within the press. However, the party held a comparatively much greater asset within its grasp – the state-run Hungarian Radio and Television. In contrast to the print media, the electronic media still remained overwhelmingly in the hands of the state. While private cable, satellite television broadcasts and independent radio stations had made inroads into Hungary since the late 1980s, state-run television and radio still dominated the airwaves, with private broadcasts lagging far behind.

The reach of the electronic media gave the government a potentially powerful tool for shaping public opinion. According to one survey, some 80 per cent of the population watched television regularly, and some 60 per cent of the population over 14 listened to radio. Both served as an important source of news, much greater than the print media as a whole.[12]

Thus, given the nature of the transition in Hungary, the dispersal of power between the government and opposition, and the position of the press, it is in retrospect not surprising that the government should view the state electronic media as a significant 'military position' (to use the MDF's own term) to bolster its power. While the so-called 'media war' in radio and television flared into open conflict in 1992, signs of this struggle could already be seen in 1990; in fact, attempts to prevent such a battle served to worsen it. Even prior to open parliamentary elections, in early 1990 a transitional presidency was created to oversee Hungarian Radio and Television, staffed by a number of MDF supporters. This board almost immediately upon its formation dismissed Endre Aczél, chief editor of the daily and weekend television news programmes. Aczél was then replaced by presidency member István G. Pálfy, known primarily for his orientation toward the MDF than for any experience in electronic media. Aczél's dismissal was justified by the argument that he had been too close to the old regime; however, the 'old regime', though now reformed since the transformative October congress, still remained in power. Why then should the Socialists seek to give greater control over the government media to the conservative opposition prior to elections?

The answer appears to be that the ruling MSZP, its popularity on the wane despite organizational, ideological and personnel changes, was involved in private negotiations with the MDF, which was expected to gain the greatest share of votes in the forthcoming elections among the various opposition parties. Hoping to divide political power between themselves and the MDF, the Socialists apparently saw giving the MDF some control over the media as a way of securing their support.[13] Other opposition parties, particularly the liberal SZDSZ, condemned this action, fearing that even prior to elections the electronic media would turn into a political instrument, subject to direct control by whichever parliamentary group was currently in power.

While parliamentary elections in the spring of 1990 foiled MSZP hopes to hang on to power, the future role of the state-run electronic media in the new political order still remained unresolved. The new MDF government now held direct control over Hungarian Radio and Television, but in parliament it was paralysed by constitutional provisions left over from the old regime that prevented the passing of legislation without a two-thirds majority – something the ruling coalition did not hold. To overcome this barrier, the government would have to modify the constitution, and to do so it needed the help of the largest opposition party, the liberal SZDSZ.

The pact which resulted from MDF–SZDSZ negotiations cleared the way for a simple majority vote for most legislation. However, a number of sensitive areas were left with a two-thirds requirement for passage, among them laws on the media. As it was understood, government and opposition would begin immediate work on a new media law to replace that left over from the socialist era, governing the powers and status of the electronic media and setting parameters for the introduction of market forces and private ownership. Until that time, a moratorium on broadcasting licences was instated, inadvertently freezing the dominance of state-run radio and television over the Hungarian airwaves.[14]

An additional outcome of the pact regarded the status of the office of the president, which too reflected the nature of the transition and its institutional origins. By 1988 the communist party began to seek a way to reorganize and maintain power in the face of domestic and international pressure. This manifested itself in an attempt by the ruling communists to create a strong presidency independent of parliament prior to free elections in the hope of gaining this office for themselves. Although the attempt was blocked, the institutional architecture of the office and its powers remained in place, and its method of election was left ambiguous. In their pact the MDF and the SZDSZ agreed to designate the office as one directly elected by parliament, expecting to relegate it to a largely ceremonial status; in return for their support, an SZDSZ candidate, Árpád Göncz, was supported by the government for the post. Other features of the office were left intact. Later, as the media war would intensify, the MDF would come to regret this move.[15]

Finally, the MDF–SZDSZ pact specified that the transitional presidency governing Hungarian Radio and Television would be replaced by appointments acceptable to both government and opposition, who would hold these positions until new media legislation was passed. Chosen as president of Hungarian Television and Radio were Elemér Hankiss and Csaba Gombár, respectively, both noted sociologists who enjoyed widespread parliamentary support. The expectations were that Gombár and Hankiss would fill these posts for no more than a year, by which time the new media law would be in effect.[16]

With these actions it appeared as though the government and opposition had stepped back from a potentially explosive situation by creating mechanisms to insulate the broadcast media from the parliamentary battles. But these mechanisms quickly broke down as acrimony grew between the conservative government and the combined liberal and socialist opposition. In essence, all parties had underestimated the difficulty in creating a new media law; opposition forces hoped to use the law to insulate the electronic media as much as possible from the (current) government's influence, while the government hoped to use its powers to purge radio and television of their communist-era staffs and reporters, to be replaced with individuals more 'objective' and friendly to the government. Moreover, few of those involved in the legislative process had any practical experience with the media. With parliament deadlocked, no legislation emerged.[17]

As relations between government and opposition worsened, the ruling coalition (particularly the MDF) felt itself under constant attack by the press for its inexperience and its conservative viewpoints. The government viewed this press criticism as a clearly biased ideological attack disguised as journalism.[18] It responded with its own supporters inside the state-run media, such as television news editor-in-chief Pálfy, to counter with pro-government reporting. In turn, journalists in radio and television who opposed such government interference used their positions to criticize the government even more vigorously. Radio and television programmes thus began to diverge widely depending on whether their editorial staffs favoured or opposed the government, leading to radical shifts in political outlook depending on the day, the channel or the programme.[19]

For their part, Gombár and Hankiss attempted to block any further influence by the government in the broadcast media and resisted organizational and programming changes that the government favoured, only further increasing the antagonism between the two sides. The government finally sought to break this stalemate by forcing Hankiss and Gombár from power, arguing that under their direction the broadcast media had fallen in 'alien hands' that did not truly represent Hungarian national values.[20] In early 1992 Prime Minister Antall appointed László Csúcs and Gábor Nahlik as vice-presidents of Hungarian Radio and Television, respectively, despite arguments by the opposition parties that such appointments were unacceptable without a new media law. Both soon set about implementing changes at these two institutions in accordance with the government's objectives. In the case of Hungarian Television, Nahlik went so far as to initiate a radical reorganization of the budget, staff and content of Hungarian Television only two days after taking office, and without the consultation or presence of Hankiss, who was out of the country. Upon his return Hankiss revoked Nahlik's orders and initiated disciplinary proceedings against him. The government similarly used budgetary instruments to deprive Hungarian Radio and Television of necessary funds, and launched various attacks against the editors of particular programmes which were viewed as excessively critical of the government (such as *168 Óra*).[21]

By May the government moved to dismiss Hankiss and Gombár officially. Prime Minister Antall first ordered Gombár's removal, after parliamentary hearings (which neither Gombár nor the parliamentary opposition attended) accused him of political bias. Lacking a new media law which would give the government the right to dismiss or appoint the media presidents, the prime minister fell back on a 1974 decree which gave the government this power. The dismissal was then sent to be countersigned by President Göncz, as constitutional provisions dictated.

At this point Przeworski's 'traces of extrication' – the remnants of the old regime's attempt to create a strong presidential office – surfaced to complicate matters. Göncz refused to countersign the dismissal, citing his right to do so in the constitution, should it be necessary to defend the democratic functioning of the political system. In Göncz's argument, the removal of Gombár threatened press freedom. The opposition rallied to Göncz's side, while coalition parties accused him of overstepping his authority. The government and opposition now appealed to the Constitutional Court, asking for clarification of the powers of the president, and the constitutionality of the 1974 decree. The court found the 1974 decree unconstitutional, but allowed it to remain in force until new media legislation was passed – which the court demanded by the end of November. With regard to the president, the court refused to delimit the president's power clearly, restating only that Göncz was obliged to countersign governmental appointments unless they did not fulfil the necessary legal conditions or they represented a threat to the democratic functioning of the state.

The government viewed the court's ruling as a victory; so did the president. In late June 1992 the prime minister resubmitted Gombár's removal, now adding Hankiss to the list. Göncz again refused, taking advantage of the court's ambiguous ruling in his regard, reiterating that without a new media law, the removal of Hankiss and Gombár would place too much media power in the hands of the government. The government appealed to the court to tighten its ruling with regard to the president, but the court, unwilling to become further entangled in this struggle, declined.[22]

The battle lines were now clearly drawn between government and opposition, prime minister and president. Hankiss and Gombár, meanwhile, continued to resist government encroachment on their positions even as pressure against them increased. In September Hankiss fired editor-in-chief Pálfy from his position as head of television news, charging him with political bias in his reporting; in October he also suspended the pro-government Alajos Chrudinák from his position as editor of the documentary news programme *Pánorama* (both were subsequently restored to their posts by court decisions). For its part the government, having failed through standard channels to remove the media heads, turned to other methods. In late November the government charged Hankiss and two of his deputies at Hungarian Television with financial mismanagement and impropriety, charges which later proved unfounded. The deadline for the new media legislation also came and went. A compromise draft bill, submitted to parliament in December 1992, became so entangled in political disputes that in the end it did not even garner a single vote.[23]

By early 1993 both Hankiss and Gombár had had enough. In January the two presidents of Hungarian Television and Radio stepped down, asking the president to be relieved of their positions. Göncz still refused even these requests, leaving their termination unclear. Despite these ambiguities the absence of Hankiss and Gombár meant that vice-presidents Nahlik and Csúcs were free to act in their stead. With the final obstacles removed, the government now used Nahlik and Csúcs to remake the electronic media in their own image.[24]

## The Government Gains Control

In accordance with our opening arguments, the purge within the electronic media which followed Hankiss's and Gombár's removal cannot simply be characterized as the product of an authoritarian-leaning government which sought to stifle objective journalism. While such criticism may be valid, it is a much more accurate and valuable observation that in fact the new government found itself influenced by the institutional context surrounding it. For the post-communist coalition government, this translated into an independent press whose ideological neutrality was doubtful, electronic media inherited largely intact from the old order, and the existence of constitutional provisions and a strong opposition which could block government policies. In these circumstances, it is not surprising that the government eventually reverted to questionable tactics to redress the situation.

As the new heads of Hungarian Television and Radio, Nahlik and Csúcs moved rapidly during 1993 to initiate wide-ranging changes in the staffing and content of the electronic media. In both cases, this reorganization led to the reintroduction of a more hierarchical control over staff, and foresaw the elimination of many political programmes, to be replaced with a greater emphasis on entertainment. The removal of such programmes, given their high levels of popularity and frequent criticism of the government, was clearly seen by many observers as an attempt by Nahlik and Csúcs to eliminate anti-government programming from radio and television.[25]

By the autumn, the physical removal of journalists and programmes unacceptable to the government began. Csúcs suspended the radio programme *Reggeli Krónika* on 25 October, blaming the programme's lack of objectivity.[26] At Hungarian Television the following day, the evening news programme *Egyenleg* also came under attack for a broadcast the previous October, when it had reported that skinheads had disrupted a speech by President Göncz commemorating the 1956 revolution, during which the police did not intervene. Nahlik claimed that the programme had falsified the footage, and he suspended *Egyenleg*'s editor and three of his colleagues, leading the remaining staff to quit the programme (the charges were later determined to have been unfounded).[27] Several new appointments to important positions at Hungarian Television and the national press agency MTI also drew criticism from the opposition members of parliament as clearly based on partisan considerations.[28]

By November, President Göncz was warning in an interview with the Italian paper *La Stampa* that press freedom was in serious danger in Hungary.

By the end of 1993, the government and its appointments could claim successes on the media front. Reorganization within Hungarian Television and Radio had brought programming and journalists under central control; the television news, returned to Pálfy's control after Hankiss's unsuccessful attempt to fire him, was solidly in the government's corner, and several critical programmes had been silenced. But at what cost? The government's strong-arm tactics had generated both domestic and international criticism, and this threatened to damage the coalition's popularity, particularly that of the MDF. According to one domestic opinion poll, by late 1993 nearly 27 per cent of those surveyed responded that they did not trust the radio and television at all, compared with 18 per cent for the print media.[29] With elections less than a year away, government influence within the media as a whole would now be put to the test.

## Government, Media, and the 1994 Elections

In December 1993 Prime Minister Antall died after a long battle with cancer. His successor, the MDF leader Péter Boross, faced the difficult task of taking control of government and also preparing for elections in the following spring. The government coalition fared poorly in opinion polls, while opposition parties, notably the MSZP, were gaining popularity. Faced with this threat, the government turned to its increased control over the media as a way to recapture support and discredit the opposition.

The removal of critical elements within the electronic media continued. In April 1994 the radio programme *Gondolat-jel* was cancelled by Csúcs on the basis of its purported bias.[30] Even more dramatically, in March Hungarian Radio summarily dismissed 129 journalists from their posts. While it was widely acknowledged that both radio and television were over-staffed, the choice of these cuts was clearly political; Csúcs himself acknowledged that dismissals were based on whether, in the eyes of the government, those sacked had been previously associated with the previous communist regime.[31] One of the most seriously hit programmes in this purge was the long-running news programme *168 Óra*, which lost its editor and many of its staff.

With these final acts of political consolidation, the government turned the broadcast media squarely against the opposition. Initially this took the form of shutting out information which would give exposure to opposition forces or their criticisms of the government. According to a study by the Hungarian media public interest group Nyilvánosság Klub, by late 1993 news coverage within Hungarian Television and Radio had become strongly biased in favour of the government and against the opposition. With the suspension of *Egyenleg* especially, opposition parties and figures – particularly the MSZP – were underrepresented in news coverage, even as their popularity increased, and coverage regarding domestic problems declined in favour of positive presentation of the government's successes or simply neutral coverage of innocuous events (following the wisdom that no news is good news).[32] As one observer put it, 'months go by without the viewers being able to watch a debate in which representatives of parties holding contrasting views are participating'.[33]

As elections drew nearer, the government fell back on more direct methods of open condemnation, centring the worst of these attacks on the MSZP. Following its creation out of the ashes of the old communist party and its poor showing in 1990 elections, the party had staged an amazing comeback, garnering the greatest popular support already in late 1993, even as the MDF's popularity eroded.[34] As a later report (again by the Nyilvánosság Klub) indicated, by spring broadcast coverage of the MSZP did increase, although it still lagged behind coverage of smaller parties that were seen as potential coalition allies of the MDF. In addition, much of this new coverage was in the form of criticism of the MSZP, rather than presentation of their own views.[35] Opposition parties began to charge that a fair election could not occur given that the electronic media 'openly belong to the government' and are clearly biased in their electoral coverage.[36]

As the government grew more fearful of elections, this criticism went to extreme lengths, combining both press and broadcast media power into a single barrage. The broadcast media had earlier been carrying oblique reports which suggested that an MSZP victory would be tantamount to a return of communist power. But by late April, the pro-government newspaper *Pesti Hírlap* began an open attack on the MSZP. Its editor, András Bencsik (who was also running as an MDF candidate for parliament) stated at a public rally that the MSZP's president, Gyula Horn, was 'certainly a criminal and possibly a murderer', claiming that the party president had been active in the suppression of the 1956 revolution. Bencsik's assertion was then duly reported by his own paper. Several days later the television documentary programme *Pánorama* broadcast a long report detailing Bencsik's charges, claiming that during the revolution Horn had brutally assaulted a hospitalized revolutionary. The paper *Új Magyarország* also raised the charge, while *Pesti Hírlap* printed excerpts from the television programme.[37]

As a final salvo, just days before the election, television news chief editor István Pálfy, speaking on the popular weekend news programme *A Hét*, implored his viewers to vote against the liberal or socialist opposition, for such a victory for the 'liberal–bolshevik alliance' would lead to the destruction of the Hungarian people and, bizarrely, their replacement through the mass resettlement of foreigners.[38] Although the National Election Committee, charged with supervision of the parliamentary campaign, enjoined the electronic media to observe impartiality, media representatives countered that the broadcast media were not electoral organs and thus not subject to the authority of the NEC.[39]

In the end, the government's media influence failed to save it. The elections in the spring of 1994 produced an overwhelming victory for the MSZP, which formed a parliamentary coalition with the SZDSZ that gave them 72 per cent of the seats in parliament. The MDF, in contrast, lost most of its seats. While this poor showing can to a large extent be attributed to the handling of economic reforms since 1990, several observers suggested that the party's attempts to conquer the media in fact damaged, rather then bolstered, its popularity. Through their actions, the government gave the impression of seeking media control at the cost of democracy, and their last-ditch attacks on the MSZP only reinforced an image of desperation.[40]

## A New Government but an Old Pattern?

We have argued above that the nature of the communist order in Hungary and the manner of its collapse to a great extent shaped media politics after 1989. With the change of government in 1994, it was unclear how this new coalition would deal with the media structure that the MDF and its allies had sought to conquer. To many domestic and Western observers, the threat to the free press in Hungary emanated from the conservative values of the MDF coalition, unwilling to brook any criticism; with this threat removed, the media in Hungary were again safe.

And indeed, with the end of the MDF coalition their conservative media battery quickly collapsed. *Új Magyarország*, the flagship of the government newspapers, was on the brink of bankruptcy when it was sold off to a private investor, who promised to moderate its tone.[41] The pro-government papers *Pest Megyei Hírlap* and *Pesti Hírlap* also ceased publication, the latter shortly after the elections. The MDF's one attempt to escape with some of its media influence intact, by selling *Magyar Hírlap* to a conservative domestic investor, was blocked by the new ruling coalition.[42]

Similar changes followed in television and radio. The former heads Nahlik and Csúcs were dismissed by the lame-duck MDF prime minister shortly after elections, as part of a deal with the incoming government to protect the two individuals from any legal charges of mismanagement. News editor István Pálfy, who continued to use the television news to attack the MSZP and SZDSZ following their electoral victory, was also finally fired by Nahlik prior to his own dismissal.[43]

Yet the new coalition's treatment of the media quickly came into question as well. In late July 1994 the government submitted new candidates to head Hungarian Television and Radio. This occurred without consultation with the opposition parties, despite government promises to do so, and also without notification of Gombár and Hankiss, who still technically remained presidents of their respective institutions. This action naturally drew widespread criticism from the opposition, as well as from Hankiss himself. The opposition appealed to President Göncz again to refuse to countersign the appointments, given that a new media legislation was still pending (the reason Göncz had refused the previous government's appointments), but this time Göncz chose to countersign the order.[44]

This initial action on the part of the new government raised fears that events during 1989–94 had set up a vicious circle. Given the penetration of the media by the previous government, the new coalition would now seek to purge those institutions and re-staff them with more sympathetic individuals, creating in essence a spoils system linked directly to the government. Further events only deepened these fears. Despite the SZDSZ and MSZP's criticism of the previous government for its anti-democratic manipulation of the media, it appeared that now in power the Left was ready to do the same.

By the autumn, evidence in this regard had mounted, as the government purged numerous individuals from various positions in television, radio and the state-run press. Many of these cuts were justified as necessary redundancies – the same argument used by the MDF – but, as with the previous government, the question was less the numbers of those dismissed, rather who they were. Within a day of taking office, the new president of Hungarian Television fired over 170 members of the staff working for the evening news (which had been known for its conservative tone under Pálfy), retaining only 20. Thus, as one observer noted, in the course of one day the new government had fired more individuals in the media than had the previous regime in four years.[45]

A scathing report in September by the conservative Community of Hungarian Journalists outlined further cuts in television and radio. In television, political and news programmes such as *A Hét* and *Pánorama* saw some or all of their staffs reassigned; at Hungarian Radio a number of higher-level managers also were removed from their posts.[46]

Even new appointments have not been safe from the government's ire. János Bethlen, hired to replace István Pálfy as head of television news, was himself fired in May 1995 after less than a year in the post. According to Bethlen and others, his dismissal resulted from what the government saw as excessive criticism of its actions in the news, rather than the media acting as a mouthpiece of the government. Domestic and international media organizations now argued that the new government's policies towards the media were in fact little different from those of its predecessor.[47]

### Overcoming the Institutional Context

The conditions laid out by the transition from communism, which led the first government to exert pressure on the media, now raise the threat that this pattern will become the new institutional form. The polarization of the media as a result of the transition has now turned that area into an instrument of political consolidation, sought by all sides in their struggle for power. Can this pattern be overcome?

In the print media, the prospects have improved for a more objective and independent press. As regards state influence, most of those papers created by the previous regime to counter the private media have collapsed, and the new government is divesting itself of those state-held press assets which remain. There is still the more complicated question of press objectivity, however, and journalistic professionalism. Given the eventual turnover of staff remaining from the socialist period and the continuing creation and development of new educational programmes for journalists, the formation of an objective, less-ideological press shows promise, but only in the long term. How the press will act in support of democracy in the interim is less clear.

With regard to the electronic media, the key issue is a new media law. If independence in the electronic media can be created through legislation which will separate the lines of authority, then television and radio may avoid becoming simply spoils, to be purged and reordered with every change of government. Initially the coalition's efforts in the area of legislation indicated that the views of the opposition would be largely ignored, raising the spectre that changes in the media law would serve primarily to consolidate governmental power.[48] As Przeworski has succinctly noted (warned?), such 'institutions that ratify a transitory advantage are likely to be as durable as the conditions that generate them'; any such changes, therefore, were unlikely to bring the battle over the media to an end.[49]

In late 1995, however, new media legislation was passed by parliament which would partially privatize the electronic media and give those portions still under state ownership more autonomy. Under this legislation, several supervisory boards will be established over the remaining segments of state radio and television, with their members chosen by government, opposition and various public interest organizations.[50] Such a compromise seems unlikely to depoliticize the media, as the various parties now seek to place partisan figures into these supervisory bodies. The International Press Institute and the European Media Institute have already criticized the new legislation as over-complicated and prone to political factionalization.[51] Whether this division of power between government and opposition will serve to balance out or further polarize the relationship between the media and politics remains unclear. An answer will have to wait until these new organizations become institutionalized into the larger political context.

## NOTES

1. Elemér Hankiss, *East European Alternatives* (Oxford: Clarendon, 1990), p.95.
2. For details see Slavko Splichal, *Media Beyond Socialism* (Boulder, CO: Westview, 1994), pp.37–9; Gábor Juhász, 'Sajtópiaci változások', in Sándor Kurtán, Péter Sándor and László

Vass (eds.), *Magyarország politikai évkönyve 1994* (Budapest: Demokrácia Kutatások Magyar Központja Alapítvány, 1994), pp.255–63, and Edith Oltay, 'The Hungarian Press Struggles to Survive', *Radio Free Europe/Radio Liberty Research Report* (hereafter *RFE/RL Research Report*), 1 Oct. 1993, pp.50–53.

3. For the full text of an internal report by the MDF parliamentary head Imre Kónya which deals in part with the media, see 'Kónya Imre tanulmánya', in Sándor Kurtán, Péter Sándor and László Vass (eds.), *Magyarország politikai évkönyve 1992* (Budapest: Demokrácia Kutatások Magyar Központja Alapítvány-Economix RT., 1992), pp.759–66.

4. *IPI Report* (Dec. 1991), pp.13–14.

5. Zoltán Farkas, 'Állóháború', in Sándor Kurtán, Péter Sándor and László Vass (eds.), *Magyarország politikai évkönyve 1991* (Budapest: Ökonómia Alapítvány-Economix RT, 1991), p.208.

6. Oltay, 'The Hungarian Press Struggles to Survive', p.51.

7. Juhász, 'Sajtópiaci változások', pp.257–8.

8. Ibid., pp.258–9.

9. Oltay, 'The Hungarian Press Struggles to Survive', p.53.

10. Ibid.

11. Lajos Biro, 'A média, a közönség, és a politika', in *Magyarország politikai évkönyve 1994*, p.699.

12. Ibid., p.702.

13. See Endre Aczél's own account of these events in *Híradó Puccs* (Budapest: Mai Nap, 1990); also Farkas, 'Állóháború', pp.207–8.

14. 'A paktum', in *Magyarország politikai évkönyve 1991*, pp.428–9.

15. For details of the role of the Hungarian presidency in the post-communist period see Patrick O'Neil, 'Political Transition and Executive Conflict in Hungary: The Balance or Fragmentation of Power?', in Ray Taras (ed.), *The Post-Communist Presidencies* (Cambridge: Cambridge University Press, forthcoming).

16. Judith Pataki, 'Power Struggle over Broadcasting in Hungary', *RFE/RL Research Report*, 12 March 1993, p.17.

17. Ibid.

18. See the interview with Prime Minister Antall, 'No One is Happy with a Distorting Mirror', *IPI Report* (June/July 1992), pp.3–4.

19. Nick Thorpe, 'TV's Rival Men of Influence', *IPI Report* (Feb. 1992), p.18.

20. Edith Oltay, 'Hungarian Radio and Television under Fire', *RFE/RL Research Report*, 24 Sept. 1993, p.41.

21. Bart Gijsbers, 'Politikai televízió és televíziópolitika', in Kurtán, Sándor and Vass, *Magyarország politikai évkönyve 1993*, pp.175–84.

22. For excerpts from various rulings, statements and letters between those parties involved in this debate see 'Médiavita: a levelezések éve', in Kurtán, Sándor and Vass, *Magyarország politikai évkönyve 1993*, pp.185–205.

23. Pataki, 'Power Struggle over Broadcasting in Hungary', pp.18–19.

24. For the text of Hankiss and Gombár's joint statement on their resignations see *IPI Report*, Feb. 1993, p.6.

25. Robert Bonte-Friedheim, 'Journalists Still Treated as Cannon Fodder', *IPI Report*, Aug. 1993, pp.16–19.

26. 'Tizenkét hónap krónikája', in *Magyarország politikai évkönyve 1994*, p.309.

27. Ibid., p.311.

28. See the report by the Nyilvánosság Klub, 'Jelentés az MR és az MTV hírműsorairól', in Kurtán, Sándor and Vass, *Magyarország politikai évkönyve 1994*, p.602.

29. Marton Kozak, 'Backfiring Propaganda: Radio and TV Remain the Citizen's Main Source of Information', *Figyelő*, 31 March 1994, p.19, translated in *Foreign Broadcast Information Service: East Europe (FBIS)*, 29 April 1994, p.11.

30. Budapest Kossuth Radio Network, 20 April 1994; *FBIS*, 21 April 1994, p.14.

31. Peter Elam, 'Hoist by its Own Media', *Index on Censorship*, July–Aug. 1994, p.21.

32. 'Jelentés az MR és MTV hírműsorairól', pp.596–607.

33. Kozak, 'Backfiring Media', p.11.

34. László Bruszt and János Simon, 'Az Antall-korszak után, a választások előtt', in Kurtán, Sándor and Vass, *Magyarország politikai évkönyve 1994*, p.793.
35. 'Impact of Pro-Government "Bias" of Media Viewed', *FBIS*, 28 June 1994, p.19.
36. See the joint statement of the SZDSZ and FIDESZ as reported by Budapest Kossuth Radio Network, 1 March 1994; *FBIS*, 3 March 1994, p.13.
37. 'Pro-Government Media Attack Horn's Past', *FBIS*, 13 May 1994, p.8.
38. Elam, 'Hoist by its Own Media', p.21; see also Ian Traynor, 'Latest Twist in Media War as Radio and TV Heads are Removed', *IPI Report*, July–Aug. 1994, p.24. The foreigners to whom Palfy refers are presumably Jews; an earlier article by Tibor Franka in the conservative *Új Magyarország* spoke of a conspiracy to allow Ukrainian Jews to resettle in Hungary: see István Nagy Igloi, interview by Lajos Kovács, 'There is a Need for Conservative Newspapers – The Media Director of *Új Magyarország*'s New Owner Argues', *Népszabadság*, 3 Feb. 1995, p.14; *FBIS*, 6 Feb. 1995, p.15.
39. MTI (Budapest), 3 May 1994; *FBIS*, 3 May 1994, p.4.
40. Kozak, 'Backfiring Media', pp.11–12; Elam, 'Hoist by its Own Media', p.21.
41. Nagy Igloi, 'There is a Need for Conservative Newspapers', p.13.
42. Rick Bruner, 'Cash-Strapped Print Journalists "Still Seeking Proper Role in Democracy"', *IPI Report*, Oct.–Nov. 1994), p.35.
43. Judith Pataki, 'Controversy over Hungary's New Media Heads', *RFE/RL Research Report*, 12 Aug. 1994, p.15; Traynor, 'Latest Twist in Media War', pp.24–5.
44. Pataki, 'Controversy over Hungary's New Media Heads', p.16.
45. Ibid., p.17.
46. 'Media Front; All-Around Attack; Saturation Bombing and Laser Operation; Report on Purges Implemented at the Hungarian Television and Hungarian Radio', *Új Demokrata*, 6 Oct. 1994, pp.21–3; *FBIS*, 29 Nov. 1994, pp.14–18.
47. *Hírmondó* <http://www.hix.com>, 17 and 18 May 1995; Rick E. Bruner, 'Journalists, Weary and Apathetic, Losing Fight for Freedom', *Hungary Report* <http://www.isys.hu>, 3 July 1995.
48. Pataki, 'Controversy Over Hungary's New Media Heads', p.16.
49. *Democracy and the Market* (Cambridge: Cambridge University Press, 1991), p.88.
50. *Magyar Közlöny*, 15 Jan. 1996, pp.97–140; see also 'Viharos békeidők', *HVG*, 6 Jan. 1996, pp.87–9.
51. *Hungary Report*, 19 Feb. 1996.

# The Dynamics of Media Independence in Post-Ceauşescu Romania

## RICHARD A. HALL

The development of the mass media in post-Ceauşescu Romania has displayed an alarming tendency to revert to communist methods of control and subservience. This is demonstrated by a detailed examination of how the various media have construed the events of the revolution of 1989. There is certainly a variety of opinion now expressed, including 'Ceauşescu-nostalgic' views, but even formally oppositionist newspapers have adopted the 'official' version of key features of those events, notably the role of the Securitate and its former director, General Vlad, and of the Soviet Union in the overthrow of the former regime. These factors suggest that the concept of media independence has been interpreted far too narrowly in Romania.

The Romanian media are both product and cause of the tainted and fragile character of Romania's young democracy. Undoubtedly, the most significant accomplishment in the post-Ceauşescu media has been the establishment of a sizeable component of the press that is free of state control. The importance of this accomplishment cannot be overestimated: these privately-owned publications routinely and vigorously criticize government officials and inform the public of present and past wrongdoing by them. Because of the pervasive and extremely repressive role played by the secret police apparatus of the Ceauşescu era (known as the Securitate), their reporting on the activities of the Securitate's institutional successors is particularly crucial to the cause of democracy.

On the basis of this information, most analysts use terms such as 'free' or 'independent' to describe this part of the press. They draw a sharp contrast between the independent press and the 'regime media' which are politically biased, anti-democratic and xenophobic, and which consistently engage in the disinformation and slander characteristic of the Ceauşescu media apparatus.[1] At the most fundamental level, Romania clearly suffers from the same problems in state–media relations as are seen elsewhere in Eastern Europe. But is independence from the state and its institutions enough in the political context of post-Ceauşescu Romania? Is it even the most pressing challenge facing the post-Ceauşescu media? This article

Richard A. Hall is a doctoral candidate in the Department of Political Science, Indiana University, Bloomington.

argues 'no' to both these questions. Because of the state's complete control of political and civil society institutions under communist rule and the consensus on the need for such institutions to be independent in order for democracy to survive and thrive, most analysts have considered the question of ending the state's control over these spheres as paramount. Critical as this development is, it is not the same thing as purging the media of the institutional legacy of the previous authoritarian regime. The 'independent' Romanian press is a good example of this.[2]

Because of the Securitate's role during the Ceauşescu era and its convoluted fate after the transition of December 1989, the generic concept of 'independence' employed in the analysis of post-communist change is inadequate in the Romanian case. The 'independent' press has generally been successful in achieving independence from the post-1989 regime of President Ion Iliescu and from the Securitate's institutional successors within the regime (no small feat considering that the regime has consistently and deviously tried to stifle these moves towards independence). In Romania, however, this is only half the battle. The problem is that the 'independent' press has not been able – nor apparently has it completely wanted – to establish the same degree of autonomy from all elements of the former Securitate. It is simply mistaken to assume that independence from the post-Ceauşescu state implies independence from the former Securitate. The tremendous fragmentation and competition within the former Securitate after December 1989 has ensured that these are not the same thing.

The result is that the former Securitate's influence on political behaviour is a *systemic* condition affecting all media sources regardless of ownership type (state or private), ideological orientation, or relationship to the regime. Although establishing media independence from the state is important and has not been easy in Romania because of the Iliescu regime's anti-democratic mentalities and tactics, this has not been the most intractable problem besetting the Romanian media since the transition. Instead, that problem has been the degree to which the remnants of the former Securitate continue both directly and indirectly to influence how and what those in the media report.

The extensive and enduring press coverage of the most fundamental event in recent Romanian history – the revolution of December 1989 – is our window to the incomplete independence of the 'independent' press. The independent press has reported relatively honestly and accurately about actions *against* the political opposition and independent media *since* December 1989 *by* the Iliescu regime and the Securitate's institutional successors within the regime. But when it comes to covering the critical events of December 1989 and their institutional consequences, the independent press has failed miserably.

In terms of ideological rhetoric, accounts of the December events vary greatly depending upon the political orientation of the publication in which they appear. This reflects the genuine and sharp ideological differences which divide the Romanian political spectrum. A closer look at these accounts, however, reveals a remarkable and unexpected consensus (even identicality) across the entire Romanian press regarding the *details* of exactly what happened in December 1989. These details serve to defend the overriding institutional interests of the former Securitate. They serve to revise the history of December 1989 and conveniently minimize and erase the role of the Securitate (particularly of specific directorates and units) in bloodily suppressing the uprising and resisting the ouster of Ceauşescu. They are at odds with what we understood to have happened at the time and they are demonstrably false.

It was the moralizing stance of the independent press itself which in many ways established reporting on the events of December 1989 as the 'litmus test' by which to judge the good faith of the post-Ceauşescu media. Many analysts assume that ideological rhetoric is an accurate guide to where the institutional interests of the former Securitate are being defended. Praise of the Ceauşescu era and praise of the former Securitate is evidence that a particular publication defends the institutional interests of the former Securitate out of ideological conviction. The men and women of Romania's independent press clearly do not defend the institutional interests of the former Securitate out of ideological conviction, however, but rather for reasons of personal and political practicality.

### Political Context and the Post-Ceauşescu Media

Why would the journalists of the independent press who routinely criticize the former Securitate, expose the illegal actions of its successor institutions in the regime of President Ion Iliescu, and clearly hate both old and new manifestations of this institution, defend the institutional interests of the former Securitate in the December 1989 events? Because, owing to the particular context of those events, the same story which exculpates much of the former Securitate from the bloodshed of that time succeeds in laying blame for the deaths at the door of the Iliescu regime – a regime which two general parliamentary and presidential elections since 1989 have not succeeded in removing and which those in the independent press deeply dislike. The chronic and seemingly insurmountable political weakness of the opposition to the Iliescu regime over the past six years and the financial difficulties of the independent press have left these journalists vulnerable.

Perhaps the critical factor, however, is that, although many new, young faces have entered the independent press since 1989, many of the editors and political reporters and commentators at major independent publications – in other words, those setting the agenda for the coverage of the events of December 1989 – worked in the Ceauşescu media apparatus. Given the highly totalitarian character of Ceauşescu's regime and the ubiquity of Ceauşescu's personality cult, the very act of working in the media apparatus in that era required complicitous behaviour. Constant compromise was the price of practising one's intellectual craft – the art of communication. A former high-ranking party-official-turned-dissident in the late Ceauşescu era, Silviu Brucan, has described the stifling pressures of the Ceauşescu era as follows:

> A large number of Romanian intellectuals were forced by the dictatorship to make moral compromises, therefore political ones. This totalitarian dictatorship of Ceauşescu's was so perfectly organized such that you could not publish a book, earn a doctorate, receive a promotion at the university, attend a conference, or publish an article without engaging in adulation of these two Ceauşescus, expressing one's loyalty to them, and praising them. And many Romanian intellectuals had to do this – very many.[3]

The potential opportunity given by a position in the media for providing a base from which to spread subversive ideas against the regime, and the emphasis the Securitate placed upon maintaining total control in this critical sphere, ensured that such compromise frequently involved collaboration with the Securitate. Per capita, the size of the Securitate's network of societal collaborators may have been as large as two-and-a-half times that of the infamous and ubiquitous East German Stasi.[4] Inevitably, the political sensitivity of a media position and the relatively small number of people who were employed in the Ceauşescu media meant that many media employees probably numbered among the Securitate's 700,000 collaborators in society at large.

As has been admitted by one journalist, whose status as a Securitate collaborator was revealed after 1989, the value of one's collaboration to the Securitate lay not in the information that collaborator could supply to the Securitate – the Securitate was swimming in such information – but in the very fact of that person's complicity.[5] Such complicity may not prevent dissident behaviour – then or now – but it can place bounds on it and encourage the alteration of its scope and direction. Pavel Campeanu, a Romanian sociologist and observer of the Romanian media, has perhaps summed it up best: 'Although the press is free in its relations to the authorities, it is not free from its past.'[6]

The issue of past collaboration would be as irrelevant to the current behaviour of media employees and inappropriate to an analysis of the media as it is in most of the rest of Eastern Europe, were it not for the peculiar fate of the Securitate after December 1989. Revealing their limited conception of change and their unwillingness and inability to dismantle the former Securitate completely, the leaders of the Iliescu regime avoided doing what almost every other new regime in Eastern Europe considered imperative: establishing public control over, and access to, the files of the former secret police to prevent their political use in the post-communist era. Serious as this failure to act was, the situation has been made infinitely more complex by the fragmentation of the Securitate since the fall of the Ceauşescu regime. Although the Romanian Information Service (the SRI) set up in March 1990 was the official heir to the Securitate and legally inherited the files of its predecessor, there have been many indications that it is not in control of all the files of the former Securitate or all the copies of those files.

The Iliescu regime reintegrated the bulk of the former Securitate into the structures of the new regime. Significantly, however, the events of December 1989 had produced a small but bitter cast of 'losers' among the former Securitate, who were angry at the new Iliescu regime for depriving them of their position, job and, in a few cases, liberty. Even though they had worked for the same institution, they were not necessarily all cut from the same ideological cloth. The nationalist, autonomous and anti-Russian components of Nicolae Ceauşescu's rule had appealed to Romanians who had little use for socialism and some of them had taken up positions in the former Securitate, especially in those directorates whose activities were most directly tied to issues of national security. This appears to have applied especially to those who worked in the Securitate's Fourth Directorate (its counter-military intelligence branch) which – because Ceauşescu feared that his opponents within the regime would attract Soviet support – had spent much of its time attempting to root out from the Romanian Army those suspected of having contacts with the KGB. Thus, former Securitate officers from various branches of the old institution found themselves outside the new regime's control just as Romania's nascent and extremely weak political and civil society institutions were taking shape. Many of these people had an axe to grind with the Iliescu regime.

Among the former Securitate who were reintegrated into the Iliescu regime, extensive formal and informal factionalization emerged. By 1996, there were as many as nine intelligence services within the Iliescu regime which had evolved out of the former Securitate and which were staffed largely by former Securitate officers.[7] The duplication of functions by these intelligence services and the rivalry among them has occasionally bubbled to the surface and has clearly contributed to much of the instability of the post-Ceauşescu period.[8] As power struggles have ensued in the new regime and former Securitate officers have been dismissed or have defected from it, the number of former Securitate officers not directly subordinate to organized control has increased.[9] While many former Securitate officers have little use for the individuals and democratic ideals of those in the political opposition or the independent press, they have recognized that the opposition of these groups to the Iliescu regime provides them with a vehicle through which they can settle their scores with the regime. The political and economic desperation and compromised past of many of those in the forefront of the political opposition and independent press has ensured their use as such a vehicle.

How has this fragmentation of the former Securitate affected the handling of the files of the former Securitate? The SRI maintains that between the official announcement of the disbanding of the former Securitate at the end of December 1989 and the founding of the SRI in March 1990, up to 100,000 files of the former Securitate disappeared from the Securitate's archives.[10] The Romanian press of all political colours has been flooded with documents and information over the past six years which could only have come from the archives of the former Securitate. Nicolae Ulieru, the official spokesman for the SRI (himself a former journalist during the Ceauşescu era), stated in January 1996:

> These files which are circulating through the press do not come from the SRI. There exist other possibilities for why the files of the former Securitate should circulate freely, although illegally. ... In the days of 22, 23, 24 December 1989, waves of revolutionaries poured into the headquarters of the former Securitate – you put the quotation marks where you want! From many of the Securitate's headquarters ... entire deposits disappeared from the archives, tens, hundreds and thousands of files, which later turned up you can guess where and in whose possession. Secondly, don't forget that between 24 December 1989 and 26 March 1990, the archives of the Securitate were in the custody of the Army ... Thirdly, some former employees of the Securitate exited the whirlwind of December 1989 with some files ... Fourthly, it is known with certainty that in the first months of the new regime, some among the potentates of that time profited from their position and the fact that they had access to the archives of the former Securitate and made copies of some files, which it can be presumed they use when they see fit.[11]

While Ulieru's claim that the SRI has played no role in circulating the files of the former Securitate to the press is undoubtedly false, there are strong reasons to believe he may not be lying when he claims that the SRI is not in charge of all the former Securitate's archive. Twice in the past six years, the SRI Director himself, Virgil Magureanu, has had to respond to attempts to print files showing his service as a Securitate collaborator and officer. In spring 1992, two independent weeklies, *Tinerama* and *Expres Magazin*, published documents showing Magureanu's service in the foreign intelligence branch of the Securitate between 1969 and 1972.[12] It is commonly believed that the document was given to the independent press by the former deputy prime minister and former senator Gelu Voican Voiculescu, who had headed a rival intelligence service to the SRI (Interior Ministry unit UM 0215; also staffed by former Securitate officers) until Magureanu had manoeuvred to remove him from that position of influence.[13]

In late 1995, the Ceaușescu-nostalgic publication of Corneliu Vadim Tudor, *România Mare*, which had only recently turned critical of the SRI Director, threatened to publish Securitate documents showing that Magureanu had been a Securitate informer as a student. Magureanu took the threat sufficiently seriously to preempt Vadim Tudor and released this section of his file for publication in the independent press.[14] Vadim Tudor maintained that he had been given the SRI Director's file by 'active duty and reserve generals' of the former Securitate; Magureanu himself suggested that officers of the former Securitate and those marginalized from the SRI were behind Tudor's actions.[15] After this second episode, Magureanu admitted:

> ... I can state that there is a greater possibility of people using various data, various documents, for the purpose of blackmail in extremely sensitive times such as the electoral period. This type of information has probably been stored somewhere and will be used.[16]

Magureanu is not alone in these views. Lucian Pintilie, Romania's acclaimed film-maker, argued in October 1992 that, while some of the former Securitate had gone into business or had remained in the new regime, 'others were excluded and it is these people who hold the most important files and who exercise a powerful blackmail in order to take power. All these rivalries among the diverse wings of the Securitate have a grotesque dimension to them.'[17] If even the SRI Director can be threatened with documents showing his former collaboration and is forced to take actions he would not otherwise have taken, then how is the professional behaviour of the average Romanian journalist affected by the possibility of such revelation?

### New Publications, Old Faces and 'Personnel Continuity'

Both foreign and domestic observers argue that 'personnel continuity' among staff in the regime media has a detrimental effect on reporting. Yet these same observers largely ignore the issue of 'personnel continuity' in the independent media. A look at the boards of directors, editorial boards and staff of political reporters and commentators at most major independent publications reveals that many of these people worked in the Ceauşescu media apparatus. Of course, the real issue here is not what an individual did in the past, but whether or not what a person did has affected his or her reporting or professional actions since December 1989. Let us examine the cases of two of the most prominent personalities in the Romanian independent press: Ion Cristoiu and Sorin Rosca Stanescu.

Ion Cristoiu is the media mogul of post-Ceauşescu Romania. He founded or played a major role at some of the most important opposition weeklies of the post-Ceauşescu era – *Expres*, *Expres Magazin*, and *Zig-Zag* – and is editor-in-chief of *Evenimentul Zilei*, the Romanian daily with the highest circulation since its creation in 1992. His front-page editorial each morning in *Evenimentul Zilei* captures the pulse of the opposition's views. He has been a sharp and unrelenting critic of the Iliescu regime and the SRI. *Evenimentul Zilei* has opened its doors to young people with little previous experience in journalism. Because of his criticism of the Iliescu regime and his status and influence within the independent media, foreign journalists frequently go to him for comment when they are investigating a story on Romanian politics. He is often presented as a shining symbol of the democratic media in Romania.

Cristoiu is hardly a newcomer to the world of journalism, however. Prior to December 1989, he was an important writer for a number of publications and was in charge of the 'Literary and Artistic Supplement' of the Communist Youth League daily *Scînteia Tineretului*. Why does this have relevance today? Because Cristoiu's actions since December 1989 raise questions. While his publications are filled with articles critical of the Iliescu regime and the SRI, there have been many articles which have whitewashed the role of the former Securitate in the events of December 1989. Cristoiu's publications shed light on the fact that these two trends are not mutually exclusive, but instead reflect the convoluted fate of the former Securitate and its continued influence on Romanian society.

For example, one would expect somebody of Cristoiu's democratic reputation to be highly critical of Ceauşescu's last Securitate director, General Iulian Vlad. Yet during Vlad's trial in early 1991, Cristoiu wrote articles which were surprisingly sympathetic to and supportive of General Vlad.[18] In 1993, Cristoiu stated unashamedly:

> From Westerners to Romanian dissidents, with the exception of [Silviu] Brucan, I haven't heard of people who hate Iulian Vlad. He is

a great intellectual, a refined intellectual ... I believe his arrest [in December 1989] was part of the KGB scenario. The Soviets realized that an anti-communist movement was beginning. And that it could be accelerated by the Securitate.[19]

Cristoiu's comments are unambiguous. According to him, the Securitate was a revolutionary force in December 1989 and Vlad was arrested not because of anything he had done but solely because a foreign power had wished it. 'A great intellectual, a refined intellectual', whom even dissidents do not hate, is how he describes the person Silviu Brucan has termed 'the man who headed the most brutal and monstrous repressive machinery in Eastern Europe' and – conjuring up the image of Stalin's bloody secret police director – 'our Beria'.[20]

Cristoiu's publications have also served as a haven for journalists who, after they left working for Cristoiu, have gone on to 'switch camps', so to speak, and revealed their true Ceauşescuist colours. During 1990, Angela Bacescu wrote for Cristoiu at Zig-Zag; since 1990, as a journalist for the Ceauşescu-nostalgic publication Europa, she has gained a reputation as one of the most xenophobic, anti-democratic and pro-Securitate journalists in post-Ceauşescu Romania.

Another good example is Pavel Corut, who has gained notoriety even outside Romania for the seemingly endless series of semi-fictional spy novels he has written since 1992.[21] These novels seek to rehabilitate the Securitate's reputation and rewrite the story of December 1989. They have sold surprisingly well. Forgotten now is the fact that during 1991 and 1992, Pavel Corut wrote weekly columns for Cristoiu's Expres Magazin, under either his given name or his acknowledged alias of Paul Cernescu. Corut was a high-ranking officer of the Securitate's counter-military intelligence directorate until the events of December 1989 and he even served in one of the intelligence agencies of the Iliescu regime for a short time in 1990.[22] During the summer and autumn of 1990, Corut wrote for Naţiunea, an ultra-nationalist publication that was financed by Iosif Constantin Dragan, a Romanian émigré living in Italy and well known for his neo-fascist views.[23] It is virtually unimaginable that Cristoiu did not learn of these facts before or during the two years Corut published in Expres Magazin.

Moreover, a comparison of what Bacescu and Corut wrote while working at Cristoiu's publications, and what they have written since they left, shows that the details of their stories – especially with regard to the Securitate's role in the December 1989 events – are virtually identical. The only real difference is that their nostalgia for the Ceauşescu era and xenophobia are now more open than they were in the pages of Cristoiu's publications. Cristoiu has been asked specifically about the Bacescu case.

His answer is enlightening: he argues that he realized from the beginning that Bacescu was writing to defend the interests of the former Securitate, but that, because in 1990 the Iliescu regime was claiming for itself what he maintains were unwarranted and false revolutionary merits and 'there was something true in what the Securitate was saying', he allowed her to publish.[24]

Another good example of the link between past and present can be seen in the case of Sorin Rosca Stanescu. Prior to December 1989, he wrote at *Viaţa Studentească* and *Informaţia Bucureştiului*. The latter became *Libertateă* on 22 December 1989 and Rosca Stanescu remained there for several months before transferring to the increasingly oppositional *România Liberă* in the spring of 1990.[25] Until 1994, Rosca Stanescu spent the majority of his time at *România Liberă*, where he wrote many investigative articles critical of the Iliescu regime and the SRI. He has served as the Chairman of the Romanian Journalists' Association (AZR), which groups journalists from Romania's independent press. His reputation for taking on the regime and for being the target of the regime's displeasure with his reporting encouraged foreign observers to follow his efforts to set up independent newspapers under his own direction – *Ultimul Cuvînt* and *Ziua*.[26]

During 1995, he gained attention abroad when his daily, *Ziua*, published allegations that President Ion Iliescu had been recruited by the KGB while a student in Moscow during the 1950s.[27] The General Prosecutor's Office threatened to take legal action against Stanescu's paper, prompting the organization *Reportères sans frontières* to denounce this step as an attempt at 'censorship in disguise'.[28]

Why does Stanescu's reporting merit closer scrutiny? In late April 1992, documents arrived at *România Liberă*, several other publications and foreign embassies which suggested that Stanescu and another journalist at *România Liberă* (Florin Gabriel Marculescu) had collaborated with the former Securitate. The timing was probably not accidental. Although Rosca Stanescu had been writing detailed allegations against the Iliescu regime and the SRI for over two years, the release of his file came right on the heels of an article he had written which was witheringly critical of SRI Director, Virgil Magureanu. Part of Magureanu's Securitate file had just been published in the independent press and Rosca Stanescu accused Magureanu of having lied about his past. Magureanu had apparently exacted his revenge.[29]

On 9 May 1992, Stanescu and Marculescu admitted in the pages of *România Liberă* that this information was correct. A month later, the paper's editorial board decided to release the two journalists. The editorial board claimed that the regime had pursued these two journalists specifically because they had been so critical of the regime and the SRI. Nevertheless, they had little choice but to dismiss them since otherwise the regime would use the presence of the two journalists at the daily to manipulate public opinion against *România Liberă*. The incident was so important that *The Economist* deemed it worthy of comment, presenting this as yet another example of the anti-democratic behaviour of the Iliescu regime, which was willing to use the files of the former Securitate to silence its present critics.[30]

Nevertheless, the marginalization of these journalists did not last long. After a brief stay at Cristoiu's publication, Stanescu was hired back by *România Liberă*, a little more than a year after the incident and in spite of their original rationale for having dismissed him (that his presence would damage the daily's reputation). Even though these journalists had suggested that after December 1989 the SRI had tried to contact them, virtually no one in the independent press questioned whether Stanescu's compromised background might have influenced his reporting prior to its public revelation. Certainly, few have questioned his reporting since the revelation. One Romanian political analyst, Alina Mungiu, has castigated the political opposition and independent press for their response in cases such as that of Rosca Stanescu.[31] Mungiu suggests that an opportunistic double standard leads those opposed to the Iliescu regime to 'draw an illogical difference between the "bad *securisti*" of those on the other side, whose head they demand, and those [*securisti*] who are "ours", those of the "good" world, like F.G. Marculescu, Sorin Rosca Stanescu, rehabilitated by Petre Mihai Bacanu [*România Liberă*'s senior editor] ... '[32]

It should be mentioned that Rosca Stanescu was not just any type of Securitate informant: he had collaborated for a decade (1975–85) with the Securitate's elite anti-terrorist unit (the so-called USLA) and his collaboration ended under ambiguous circumstances.[33] Ironically, in articles critical of supporters of the Iliescu regime, *România Liberă* has considered collaboration with the USLA worthy of comment and serious complicity.[34] One cannot help but conclude that one of the reasons for Rosca Stanescu's differential treatment lies solely in the fact that he opposes the Iliescu regime.

The relevance of past ties lies in whether and how they have affected reporting since the transition. In February 1991, Securitate General Iulian Vlad proposed the following scenario to explain the events which propelled Ceaușescu's ouster:

> Halfway through December 1989 massive groups of Soviet tourists began to enter the country. They entered coming directly from the USSR or from Yugoslavia or Hungary. The majority were men and – in a coordinated fashion – they deployed in a convoy of brand-new

'LADA' automobiles. In the night of 16–17 December '89 such a column attempted to enter Timişoara. Some of these cars were forced to make a detour around the town, others managed to enter it ... [35]

This 'Soviet tourist' scenario is standard fare among the former Securitate and shows up routinely in the pages of the publications of the Ceauşescu-nostalgics. Two months after Vlad's statement, however, Rosca Stanescu presented an interview in *România Liberă* in which an anonymous KGB officer residing in Paris spoke of a similar scenario.[36] In the article, Stanescu reminded his audience of 'the persistent rumours circulating referring to the existence on Romanian territory of 2,000 "LADA" automobiles with Soviet tags and two men inside each car.'[37]

He closed by asking his readers: 'Why is General Vlad being held in such an interminable checkmate? ... Is Iliescu protected or not by the KGB?'[38] In late 1994 – that is, after the revelation of his Ceauşescu-era collaboration – Stanescu published the viewpoint of a former Securitate officer which clearly implied that the Securitate could not have been responsible for the December 1989 bloodshed since at a secret meeting in November 1989 General Vlad had ordered his Securitate commanders to refrain from intervening in any street protests.[39] It is difficult to argue that in either of these cases Stanescu did not realize the dubious, if not absurd, character of these arguments and how they served the interests of the former Securitate.

### 'Solving the Mystery of December 1989': A Study in the Politics of Investigative Journalism

These examples of Sorin Rosca Stanescu's reporting suggest both the enduring interest among journalists of the independent press in the events of December 1989 and how this coverage reveals the limits of independent press autonomy. The interest of the independent press in establishing what happened during the confusing transition of December 1989 initially served a social cause. Over a thousand people had died in those events and the nation had been traumatized by the upheaval for two full weeks. The population wished to know who was responsible for the bloodshed, how the new political elite had come to power, and whether their claim to rule was legitimate. Thus, in 1990 the Romanian press was filled with constant revelations about the December events.

It can be argued that since 1990, however, the independent press's continued interest in the events of December 1989 has been a predominantly elite-driven phenomenon, something fuelled by the journalists themselves. By late 1990, the population had been so saturated by media coverage that they were confused about what to believe and cynical about whether or not the events would ever be clarified. Although coverage has dropped off steadily since 1990, the number of articles which continue to appear – more than six years after the events took place – and the attention devoted to the most minute details remains astounding. The interest of the independent press has undoubtedly been sustained by the fact that two general presidential and parliamentary elections have not dislodged the officials of the Iliescu regime who came to power during the events of December 1989. What one argues about what happened in December 1989 is thus considered to have implications for the legitimacy of the Iliescu regime throughout the entire post-Ceauşescu era.

Most analyses of the Romanian historiography of the December events suggest that there could not be a greater difference between the presentation in the independent press and accounts in regime-supportive publications. In accordance with this dichotomy, the independent press claims that Ceauşescu was ousted from power by a genuine, spontaneous popular uprising, but a coterie of *nomenklaturists* 'hijacked the revolution' – launched a pre-planned *coup d'état* – to halt the process of radical change. On the other hand, the regime-supportive press (in particular, its Ceauşescu-nostalgic component) denies or at least casts doubt upon the genuine, spontaneous and popular character of this uprising. Its journalists insinuate that the Ceauşescu regime was toppled by an international conspiracy, including a coalition of any of the following: the KGB, CIA, Hungarian intelligence, and MOSSAD (Israeli Intelligence). Some of those who came to power in December 1989 were working for this conspiracy, others (such as Iliescu) saved Romania from the conspiracy's achieving its ultimate goal: the destruction of Romania's independence.

On a rhetorical level such accounts appear very different, but a closer look at the details argued in these competing accounts reveals a surprising degree of consensus. This becomes clear when we examine the most important controversy of the December events: the question of the so-called 'terrorists'. 'Terrorists' was the name given to those who opened fire on the evening of 22 December after Nicolae and Elena Ceauşescu had been forced to flee the capital in the face of huge demonstrations. They caused great confusion and death during the following few days. During that period, approximately 22–27 December, about 900 people died, almost a third of them army personnel. Who were the terrorists? Whose side were they fighting on? Did they exist at all? What happened to them? Silviu Brucan, who played a critical role in the December events, has described the bizarre disappearance of the 'terrorists' as follows:

> The question of who the terrorists were sums up the most incredible

and queer facet of the Romanian revolution. Even more bewildering is the fact that not even historians of the future will ever be able to clear it up. All traces have disappeared for all practical purposes, and not one single terrorist is available for questioning or trial ... Everybody knows the terrorists in Romania were shooting and killing people, but not a single one of them can now plead guilty or not guilty. They are simply missing as such, although as living persons they might function as respectable entrepreneurs or businessmen, superior officers or cabinet ministers.[40]

At the time of the events, there was little debate about whether the 'terrorists' existed. They were Securitate officers fighting to gain the release of the Ceauşescus (who had been captured after trying to flee the capital). A high-level Securitate defector living in the United States and Western diplomats based in Bucharest pointed the finger in one direction: at the men of the Securitate's Fifth Directorate (charged with the protection of the Ceauşescus) and, more specifically, those of its closely affiliated 'special unit for anti-terrorist warfare' – the USLA.[41] Since December 1989, several key officials who were part of the first post-Ceauşescu government but were marginalized from power during early 1990 – including Silviu Brucan and Army General Nicolae Militaru – have corroborated this account.[42] Nevertheless, more than six years after those events, the independent press consistently maintains that the 'terrorists' were an 'invention' of those who took power in order to give their seizure of power revolutionary legitimacy. The members of the USLA have long since disappeared from the picture as suspects in the December bloodshed. The problem is that this also depicts the views expressed by journalists in the pro-regime and pro-Ceauşescu press, by former Securitate officers and by the SRI. The case study of a single, much-commented-upon incident from the December events will illustrate this unnatural and questionable consensus.

### 'The Defence Ministry Incident': What a Single Case Can Tell Us

One of the most frequently cited and controversial incidents of the Romanian Revolution occurred on the night of 23–24 December 1989 in front of the defence ministry in the capital, Bucharest. Ion Iliescu and the other officials who seized power after the Ceauşescus fled the capital on 22 December were at this hour using the ministry as the headquarters of the new National Salvation Front government. The gunfire which had erupted nation-wide from the evening of 22 December reached its peak on this night. In the midst of the chaos, seven USLA officers were gunned down as their armoured vehicles arrived at the heavily fortified defence ministry.

Among the seven dead were two of the USLA's highest-ranking officers, Lieutenant-Colonel Gheorghe Trosca, Chief-of-Staff of the USLA, and Major Eugen Cotuna, Commander of the USLA's Special 'Intervention' sub-unit.

At the time, the Romanian media reported this incident as a 'terrorist attack' – a desperate attempt by drugged, fanatical Ceauşescu loyalists to eliminate the political and military leaders of the new government gathered inside the building.[43] The media coverage of this event since December 1989 prompts three observations: (1) there has been widespread and persistent revisionism in the reporting of this incident; (2) the interpretation of this incident by former Securitate officers, by journalists of the pro-Ceauşescu press, and by journalists of the independent media is virtually identical; and (3) there exists sufficient evidence that we can reasonably disprove the revisionist explanation.

Even President Ion Iliescu pauses to discuss this incident in his 1993 book entitled *Revoluţie şi Reforma*.[44] Despite the original explanation of these events supplied by spokesmen for Iliescu's government, Iliescu has reconsidered and suggests an otherwise very plausible scenario: the army opened fire accidentally upon the USLA officers because of a breakdown in communication and the great confusion of those days. Yet at least two facts seem to suggest that at the time Front leaders and the army did not consider that an accident had occurred. Ceauşescu-nostalgics have complained bitterly since December 1989 that the bodies of the dead USLA officers were left out in the street for almost a week and profaned by the populace as 'terrorists' until finally Army General Victor Stanculescu ordered that they be collected and buried.[45] Moreover, those USLA officers who survived the incident maintain that they were arrested, beaten, given drug tests and interrogated inside the defence ministry after the incident by members of the Front.[46]

The official revision of the defence ministry incident began in late February 1990 when General Victor Stanculescu replaced General Nicolae Militaru as defence minister. General Stanculescu maintained that, far from being 'terrorists', the USLA had actually fought alongside the army in defence of the revolution. He argued that the USLA had not been involved in the repression of demonstrators in Timişoara and Bucharest in the week which led up to the flight of the Ceauşescus. The USLA officers killed at the defence ministry had come to aid in the defence of that building and tragically had been shot by the (still unknown) terrorists. Even at the time, this sudden about-face in the new regime's treatment of the USLA struck some foreign observers as a suspicious attempt at rehabilitating the reputation of the former Securitate.[47]

A collective letter sent in late 1990 to the pro-Ceauşescu *Democratia* by former Securitate officers proclaimed what has subsequently become the standard Securitate view of this incident: Army General Nicolae Militaru (located in the defence ministry at the time of the incident) had lured the USLA officers into an ambush and had ensured that the group was led by Colonel Gheorghe Trosca and Major Eugen Cotuna since, as former counter-military intelligence officers charged with Militaru's case, they had compromising information on Militaru's (alleged) links with the KGB.[48]

The head of the Securitate's counter-military intelligence directorate, General Vasile Gheorghe, who was arrested and imprisoned as a result of the December events, outlines an identical scenario.[49] Dumitru Popescu, a former Fourth Directorate officer, wrote to the pro-Ceauşescu *Europa* that

> Colonel Trosca was expressly solicited by General Militaru to intervene at the defence ministry on Drumul Taberei with a group of fighters to annihilate the terrorists ... [Trosca was killed] because he had worked effectively in unmasking the activities of Militaru as a KGB spy.[50]

Other former Securitate officers of various ranks and from various directorates parrot a similar story. Thus, even though the former Securitate may no longer exist as an institution, there is little question about what the institutional view of this incident is.

The independent press's coverage of this same incident is surprising. As a journalist for two publications at the heart of the independent press – *Expres* and *Tinerama* – Ilie Stoian ranks among those who have written most extensively about the 1989 events. Yet Stoian presents a familiar interpretation of the defence ministry incident: 'Militaru expressly requested that among the USLA personnel Colonel Trosca be sent ... Their murders were a consequence of the fact that Trosca possessed data about Militaru's links to the KGB.'[51] In his work, Stoian has cleared the USLA of any responsibility for the 'terrorism' of December 1989 and instead suggests that army and Front leaders were the real culprits.

Even Petre Mihai Bacanu, executive director of *România Liberă* – considered by many to be the 'conscience' of the Romanian media because of his tenacious criticism of the former Securitate and its successor institutions – has disseminated similar accounts. There is no denying that much of what Bacanu has written since 1989 has required courage or that prior to 1989 as a journalist at *România Liberă* he had suffered at the hands of the Ceauşescu regime (he was imprisoned in early 1989 for attempting to publish an illegal underground newspaper). Nevertheless, as early as March 1990, Bacanu was arguing that the USLA officers had been killed at the defence ministry by accident and he stridently denied that the USLA had taken part in the repression in Bucharest on the night before Ceauşescu fled.[52] Eyewitness accounts published immediately after the events suggest that this second claim is simply false.[53] Bacanu, who was already critical of almost any regime action, curiously was in almost total agreement with General Stanculescu's assertions.[54]

Since then Bacanu's view of this incident has only become more questionable. In December 1992, he suggested explicitly that General Militaru had appealed for the USLA to come to protect the defence ministry from the terrorists and that it was not accidental that 'Lt. Col. Trosca who had worked on the dossiers "Corbii", "Igor", and "Olga" [all relating to the KGB ties of Militaru and other Front leaders]' had been among them.[55] Significantly, Bacanu's statement came a day after *România Liberă*'s first ever interview – a full three years after the events – with Army General Nicolae Militaru. In that interview, Militaru maintained with certainty that the USLA had been the 'terrorists' and that those who had been killed in the defence ministry incident had come in attack.[56]

Since 1992, Bacanu has continued to insinuate that Colonel Trosca and the USLA officers who came to the defence ministry were lured into a trap and killed unjustly.[57] Coming as this claim does from the pen of one of Romania's most respected journalists this myth has gained a credibility with the population which it could not have attained in the pro-Ceauşescu press alone.

But is it possible that in this case the former Securitate is telling the truth and that this explains the odd convergence of accounts in the independent and pro-Ceauşescu press? This seems highly unlikely. In June 1990, in the pages of the army daily, Army Major Mihai Floca attacked what he considered to be the growing wave of revisionism in the civilian press.[58]

According to Floca,

> The fact that ever since the Revolution the Army has been the target of well-directed attacks which have become more and more insistent can be seen by anyone. Far too few of the journalists who sign such slanderous articles which appear in certain publications are still interested in what happened to the army during the Revolution. The sacrifice of 267 officers, recruits and soldiers now has little importance! All that these 'well-intentioned people' ['*oameni de bine*', a term which can imply people with Securitate ties] wish to show is how the army contributed to genocide, with the eventual goal of demonstrating that the army made the greatest contribution.[59]

Floca targeted one article in particular: an article in Ion Cristoiu's *Zig-Zag* by the above-mentioned Angela Bacescu.[60] In that article, Bacescu interviewed USLA officers who had survived the gunfight and proposed a by now familiar scenario: the USLA had been cynically lured into an ambush in order that they could be killed as 'terrorists'; in reality they had not been 'terrorists', and they were not involved in the repression prior to 22 December (they could not have been as it was not part of their duties).

Army Major Floca challenged what he considered the revisionism of the civilian press with interviews of army soldiers who had participated in the incident and of civilians who had witnessed the events of those days from the nearby apartment blocs. The comments of one army officer are telling:

> Until now I have not said much even though I was aware of the attempts of certain journalists to make the USLA into heroes. I kept quiet because I thought about those left behind by those who had fallen, wives and children who bear no responsibility for what happened. But now, since we have been accused of a crime, and since *in not a single civilian newspaper has our point of view been presented* I have the obligation to say what I saw.[61]

The interviewees supplied information which is devastating for the revisionist argument: the armoured vehicles bearing the USLA members had approached in the middle of the night with their headlights dimmed, had manoeuvred between tanks at a distance for 30 minutes without making contact with anyone, and had opened fire. Although their arrival was expected, they did not approach by the agreed route, and one of the original three armoured vehicles stopped en route. Captain Victor Stoica asks: 'If they had come with such innocent intentions, why did they stop in between the tanks rather than head straight for the ministry? Probably because – as we discovered the next morning – none of the USLA officers had on his person any identity papers ... '.[62] Reinforcing the idea that the USLA officers had arrived as if on a wartime mission was the fact that they were wearing army uniforms over their USLA insignia.

Writing in August 1990, Floca and a group of Army officers maintained that those who had related what they had seen 'have been warned to think long and hard since they have families and to stay on their own turf if they do not want to have problems'.[63] Several residents of the nearby apartment blocs have claimed that in May 1990 they were visited by former Securitate officers who informed them of the 'correct' understanding of the incidents which had taken place outside the defence ministry in December 1989.[64] Floca suggested in August 1990 that the physical 'terrorism' of December had been replaced by 'verbal terrorism' – a charge which apparently extended to the journalists of the civilian press who were making heroes of the USLA officers.[65]

These accounts suggest a great irony. At least initially, the army's victorious role in the Revolution and its ability to maintain its institutional coherence allowed it to free itself of the pervasive infiltration and manipulation of the former Securitate. Thus, when it came to covering the actions of the former Securitate in the December events, journalists in the army press performed far better than those in the civilian press – where the former Securitate was able to exert influence much more effectively.[66] The great misfortune was that few civilians read the army press.

## Conclusions: Constrained Media

How do we explain this strange consensus in erroneous reporting and interpretation to which even the independent press is a party? Silviu Brucan argues that the views expressed by former Securitate General Vlad in early 1991 – according to which no 'terrorists' had existed in December 1989 and the deaths that had occurred had been the result of army units firing into other regime forces and civilians – have come to dominate throughout the post-Ceauşescu press. According to Brucan,

> That line of argument became the favourite thesis of the entire media apparatus that used to be controlled by the famous Disinformation Department of the Securitate. There is no need for a list of informers and disinformers to be published: anyone who looks through a collection of 1991 newspapers and notes the names of those who argued and documented most aggressively the theses of General Vlad will discover the network of journalists on the take of the Disinformation Department!

> Much has been said and written about the ingenious procedures and methods used by the Disinformation Department in the service of Ceauşescu. However, that department's greatest performance by far has been achieved since the revolution because it has succeeded in creating such total confusion around the terrorists that nobody knows anything about who they were and what they did.[67]

Brucan has perhaps identified the most crucial factor at work here. Nevertheless, we should not ignore the degree to which latent fear of the former Securitate (even – perhaps especially – among its former collaborators) and the chronic weakness of political opposition to the Iliescu regime and the capital dependence of the independent press have contributed to the complicitous behaviour of these journalists. There is little doubt that these same compromised journalists of the independent press wish to be rid of the past and to see Romania's democratic experiment succeed, but their journalistic behaviour indicates that current reality is a lot more complex. More than six years after the collapse of the Ceauşescu regime, two of the principles at the heart of the democratic process –

freedom of expression and access to alternative sources of accurate information – remain constrained in Romania.

The example of the Romanian independent press suggests that the emphasis in post-communist studies upon establishing independent media free of state political and economic control and willing to criticize and investigate regime officials has been far too exclusive. One can understand the importance accorded to this goal in view of the state's dominance of the media during the communist era and given the importance of an independent media to the construction and functioning of a healthy democracy. Nevertheless, this exclusive emphasis has led to the neglect of other serious concerns and defined what 'independence' means much too narrowly.

### NOTES

1. See Dan Ionescu, 'Romania's Media Independence Struggles', *Transition*, 6 Oct. 1995, pp.52–4; Liviu Man, 'The Independent Press in Romania: Against the Grain', *Uncaptive Minds*, Vol.6, No.2 (Summer 1993), pp.89–96; Peter Gross, 'Restricting the Free Press in Romania', *Orbis*, Vol.35, No.3 (Summer 1991), pp.365–75.

2. The state's near monopoly control over television until only very recently (things are better in radio where there has been an explosion of independent local FM stations in recent years), and the Iliescu regime's heavy politicization of both state television and state radio, are not in dispute here. This situation is clearly a problem and unfortunate. The reporting by state television and radio is frequently abysmal; but this is a surprise to virtually no one. The real test of establishing free media is ultimately in that section of the media which makes claims to independence. This is where the importance of the independent press lies in Romania: if the removal of the state has still left major problems in its wake in the independent press, then the same is likely to happen in radio and television.

3. Silviu Brucan, interview by Nestor Rates, in Silviu Brucan, *Piaţă şi Democraţie* (Bucharest: Editura Stiintifică, 1990), p.55.

4. The Stasi had approximately 190,000 collaborators out of a population of 17 million; the Securitate 700,000 out of a population of 23 million. The number 700,000 is frequently cited: see, for example, Silviu Brucan, *The Wasted Generation* (Boulder, CO: Westview, 1993), p.158; or former chairman of the Liberal Party, Radu Campeanu, in 'Parlamentarii despre dosarele Securităţii', *România Liberă*, 15 May 1992, p.3.

5. Florin Gabriel Marculescu, interview by Andreea Pora, 'Nu am avut curajul să refuz colaborarea', *22*, 15–21 May 1992, p.12.

6. Quoted in the Human Rights Watch/Helsinki Report, 'Romania: Restrictions on Freedom of the Press in Romania', Vol.6, No.10 (June 1994), p.5.

7. See Dennis Deletant, 'The Securitate Legacy in Romania: Who Is in Control?', *Problems of Post-Communism*, Vol.42, No.6 (Nov.–Dec. 1995), pp.23–8.

8. Paul Stefanescu, *Istoria Serviciilor Secrete Româneşti* (Bucharest: Editura Divers Press, 1994), pp.292–4.

9. For an idea of the waves of dismissals which have occurred at the SRI see Mihail Galatanu, 'Virgil Magureanu a cîştigat batalia pentru SRI', *Expres*, 17–23 May 1994, pp.8–9.

10. Ibid.

11. Nicolae Ulieru, interview by Dana Balint, 'Războiul dosarelor nu e declansat de SRI', *Cotidianul*, 17 Jan. 1996, pp.1; 3.

12. Ioan Itu, 'Dosarul de securitate al domnului Magureanu', *Tinerama*, 27 March–2 April 1992, pp.8–9.

13. On the conflict between the SRI and UM 0215, see Deletant, op. cit., p.27. Magureanu himself believed that Voiculescu was behind the release of his file: see Sorin Rosca Stanescu, 'Securea lui Magureanu', *România Liberă*, 17 April 1992, pp.1, 3.
14. Virgil Magureanu sent his file to the independent daily *Evenimentul Zilei* on 29 December 1995.
15. L.G., 'Înaintea publicării dosarului, Magureanu il consultase pe Iliescu', *Cotidianul*, 10 Jan. 1996, p.1.
16. Virgil Magureanu, interview in *Adevărul*, 8 Jan. 1996, p.1.
17. Lucian Pintilie, interview in *România Liberă*, 21 Oct. 1992, p.5.
18. Ion Cristoiu, 'Iulian Vlad stîrneşte invidii', *Expres Magazin*, 30 Jan.–5 Feb. 1991, p.1.
19. Constantin Iftime, *Cu ION CRISTOIU prin infernul contemporan* (Bucharest: Editura Contraria, 1993), p.31.
20. Brucan, *The Wasted Generation*, p.194; Silviu Brucan, 'Cine şi de ce nu vrea 'sa-l supere pe Generalul Vlad', *Adevarul*, 29 Jan. 1991, p.2.
21. See Michael Shafir, 'Best Selling Spy Novels Seek to Rehabilitate Romanian Securitate', *RFE/RL Research Report*, 12 Nov. 1993, pp.14–18.
22. Dan Badea, 'Secretele Revoluţiei', *Expres*, 7–13 June 1994, pp.8–9.
23. See, for example, Pavel Corut, 'Dacii liberi', *Naţiunea*, August 1990, p.6.
24. Iftime, *Cu ION CRISTOIU prin infernul contemporan*, p.126.
25. *România Liberă* had existed during the communist era and its staff decided to keep the paper's name after December 1989. Although initially supportive of the Iliescu regime, by February 1990 it began distancing itself and by March 1990 it was sharply critical of it.
26. *IPI Report* (Oct.–Nov. 1993) p.18.
27. See Dan Ionescu, 'The President, the Journalists, and the KGB', *Transition*, 8 Sept. 1995, pp.36–9.
28. Ibid.
29. See Sorin Rosca Stanescu, 'Securea lui Magureanu', *România Liberă*, 17 April 1992, p.1, 3; Anton Uncu, 'Opriti-l pe Arturo Ui', *România Liberă*, 30 April 1992, p.1, 3.
30. Rosca Stanescu, 'Sint H-15', *România Libera*, 9 May 1992, p.5; 'Catre SRI', *România Liberă*, 9 June 1992, 1; 'Goodbye Magureanu', *The Economist*, 18 June 1992, cited in *Tinerama*, 10–17 July 1992, p.3.
31. Alina Mungiu, *România după '89* (Bucharest: Editura Humanitas, 1995), p.259.
32. Ibid.
33. Sorin Rosca Stanescu, interview by Andreea Pora, '"H-15" în slujba patriei', 22, 15–21 May 1992, p.13.
34. See the case of Jamal Kurbissa in *România Libera*, 23 Aug. 1995, p.16.
35. See Vlad's testimony in Mircea Bunea, 'Da sau Ba?', *Adevărul*, 16 Feb. 1991, reprinted in Mircea Bunea, *Praf in Ochi* (Bucharest: Editura Scripta, 1994), pp.460–61.
36. Sorin Rosca Stanescu, 'Iliescu aparat de K.G.B.?', *România Liberă*, 18 April 1991, p.8.
37. Ibid.
38. Stanescu's intentions are drawn further into question by the fact that Romania's supposed 'master spy', Securitate Colonel Filip Teodorescu (arrested and sentenced for his actions in Timişoara), favourably cites this very article extensively in a book on the December events: see Filip Teodorescu, *Un Risc Asumat* (Bucharest: Editura Viitorul Românesc, 1992), pp.93–4.
39. Rosca Stanescu's article from a December 1994 issue of *Ziua* was reprinted in Cornel Dumitrescu, 'Dezvaluiri senzationale despre decembrie '89', *Lumea Liberă*, 17 Dec. 1994, p.16.
40. Silviu Brucan, *The Wasted Generation*, p.183.
41. David Binder, 'Ceauşescu's "Private Army": A Force of Unabated Cruelty', *New York Times*, 25 Dec. 1989, p.A12; Blaine Harden, 'Doors Unlocked on Romania's Secret Police', *The Washington Post*, 30 Dec. 1989, p.A1, A14.
42. Brucan, *The Wasted Generation*, pp.183–6; Nicolae Militaru, interview by Corneliu Antim, 'Ordinul 2600', *România Liberă*, 17 Dec. 1992, pp.1–2.
43. Victor Dinu, 'Nimicirea Gorilelor Mercenare', *România Liberă*, 25 Dec. 1989, cited in Angela Bacescu, *România 1989: Din nou in calea navalirilor barbare* (Cluj–Napoca:

Editura 'Zalmoxis', 1994), p.151; Mihai Floca, 'Apararea Patriei', *România Liberă*, 26 Dec. 1989, cited in Dan Badea, 'Cine au fost teroristii?' *Expres*, 15–21 Oct. 1991, p.10.
44. Ion Iliescu, *Revoluţie şi Reforma* (Bucharest: Editura Enciclopedica, 1994), pp.72–3.
45. Bacescu, *România 1989*, pp.147–8; this book is a compendium of articles which first appeared in the pro-Ceauşescu weekly *Europa*.
46. Ibid., pp.151–63.
47. Mihai Sturdza, 'How Dead is Ceauşescu's Secret Police Force?', *RFE/RL. Report on Eastern Europe*, 13 April 1990, pp.33–4.
48. Group of former Securitate officers, 'Asa va place Revolutia! Asa a gost!', *Democratia*, No.36 (24–30 Sept. 1990), p.4.
49. Bacescu, *România 1989*, p.106.
50. See 'Generalul Militaru trebuie să platească', in Bacescu, *România 1989*, pp.111–12.
51. Ilie Stoian, *Decembrie '89. Arta diversiunii* (Bucharest: Editura Colaj, 1993), 37–8; this book is a collection of articles Stoian wrote for *Expres* between 1991 and 1993.
52. Petre Mihai Bacanu, 'Intercontinental 21/22', *România Liberă*, 17 March 1990, p.1.
53. Emilian David, 'Dreptate şi adevăr pentru ziua întii', *Libertatea*, 12 Jan. 1990, pp.1–2.
54. It is interesting to note that in January 1990 – before *România Liberă* had broken with the Front, and when the USLA officers killed at the defence ministry were still officially branded as 'terrorists' – Bacanu's newspaper had printed the obituaries of these fallen USLA officers under the caption 'revolutionary heroes': *România Liberă*, 9 Jan. 1990, p.4a.
55. Petre Mihai Bacanu, 'Cine a tras?', *România Liberă*, 18 Dec. 1992, pp.1–2.
56. Militaru, 'Ordinul 2600'.
57. Petre Mihai Bacanu, 'Responsabilitatea sangelui vărsăt', *România Libera*, 22 Dec. 1993, p.2.
58. Major Mihai Floca, 'Crima?!,' *Armata Poporului*, 6 June 1990, p.3.
59. Ibid.
60. Angela Bacescu, 'O crima ce trebuie neaparat dezvaluita', *Zig-Zag*, 23–9 April 1990, p.10.
61. Floca, 'Crima?!'; emphasis added.
62. Ibid.
63. Mihai Floca, 'Eroi, victime sau teroristi?', *Adevărul*, 29 Aug. 1990, pp.1–2.
64. Major Mihai Floca and Captain Victor Stoica, 'Unde sînt teroristii? Pe Strada, Printre Noi', *Armata Poporului*, 13 June 1990, p.3. It is unclear for whom these former Securitate officers were working.
65. Floca, 'Eroi, victime sau teroristi?'.
66. It should also be stated, however, that when it came to owning up to its role in the bloody repression of the demonstrators prior to 22 December, the army press (including Major Mihai Floca) was unable to admit the truth.
67. Brucan, *The Wasted Generation*, pp.194–5.

# Polarization and Diversification in the Bulgarian Press

## IVAN NIKOLCHEV

In the past six years, mass media, society and politics in Bulgaria have interacted in a complex fashion that defies separation of cause from effect. New publications were initially associated with political parties, but soon private publications appeared in a publishing boom that embraced a wide variety of genres. Former journalists of the official and institutional press played a key entrepreneurial role in the development. Shortages of newsprint and rampant inflation seriously affected the fortunes of the press, however, and this was compounded by restrictions on distribution. Furthermore, the delay in producing a law on media hindered the establishment of a well-ordered media sector. Private broadcasting has proved difficult to establish, particularly television, and supervisory procedures have been slow in being agreed.

In July 1995, the majority in the Bulgarian parliament, controlled by the formerly communist Bulgarian Socialist Party (BSP), approved a new Law on Local Elections. According to Article 62, Paragraph 1 of this law, journalists from state-owned media[1] were not allowed during the election campaign to express personal opinions or attitudes towards political parties, coalitions or individual candidates participating in the elections. The provision was immediately attacked by members of parliament from the opposition Union of Democratic Forces (UDF) and by the president of the Republic of Bulgaria. Several months later, on 13 September, the constitutional court unanimously ruled that Article 62, Paragraph 1 was unconstitutional and in conflict with international agreements signed by Bulgaria. In explaining for the decision, the judges pointed out that the provision limits the right of citizens to be informed.[2] 'Journalists', said the constitutional court chairman, Ivan Grigorov, 'are not mere recorders of events and facts; they are thinking persons.'[3] In a brief opinion article a politically moderate national daily hailed the decision, calling the repealed legal provision 'manifestly undemocratic'.[4]

A totally contradictory opinion came from the largest circulation daily, *24 Chasa* ('24 Hours'). In its editorial, the newspaper speculated that through this decision the constitutional court, generally considered to be

Ivan Nikolchev recently received his doctorate from the College of Journalism at the University of Maryland and is currently heading a USAID project on media assistance in Bulgaria.

supportive of the opposition, was favouring the ruling Socialist party. The logic was as follows: the state-owned media are under the tight control of the parliamentary majority, and therefore allowing journalists in the media to express opinions would inevitably translate into endorsement of Socialist candidates in the forthcoming local elections. It is all very well that constitutional judges stood behind freedom of speech, the editorial argued; the speech of state-owned media, however, is not free but *state speech*: it will always be on the side of the powerful.[5]

This case is a good illustration of the complex relationship between the media and politics in Bulgaria. It is an instance of one of the numerous battles in the war for control of the institutions, especially of the state-owned radio, television and the news agency. It is also an example of the lack of consensus on what journalistic professionalism, press freedom and democracy are about. It shows, albeit in a simplified way, how politics and its power struggles influence the media, and how the various media are struggling to influence politics and the society.

## Freedom of Speech and Press Under Communism

Both Bulgarian Constitutions under communist rule (adopted in 1947 and 1971) proclaimed the freedom of speech and of the press as a fundamental right. However, 'freedom' in these texts meant something completely different from what a Westerner might imagine. Journalists were assigned a special and important role: they were required to be, according to Lenin, the collective agitator, propagandist and organizer of the masses.

Naturally, the exercise of this kind of freedom could not be left to journalists alone. Although there was no press law and no official censorship, all mass media were under the direct control of the party-state. For this purpose, a special press department at the Central Committee of the Communist Party was charged with supervisory functions, such as the appointment of editors-in-chief and other key persons in the mass media. Even for lower-level positions, there was a limitation: no one could be promoted to the rank of department head (or higher) in a mass medium without being a member of the communist party.

Straying from the party line or even failing to note a politically sensitive error could (and usually would) be severely punished. Journalists were also subjected to an elaborate system of instruction by party officials and of rewards for loyal service. And it goes without saying that each and every mass medium was closely watched by a specially assigned secret service officer. As a result of all this, journalists had well learned the art of self-censorship.

Still, cracks in the system could be found. Dissenting journalists had learned the Aesopian language and the difficult skill of writing between the lines. For their part, intelligent readers had developed an ability to read between the lines. Journalists from *Orbita* – a weekly popular science newspaper published by the Communist Youth League – remember the times when they were not allowed to write about the achievements of Western science and technology. To get around this, they would describe a certain development but not attribute it to any specific country, institution or scientists: readers would have to guess its origins.[6]

Almost all Western publications were banned (exceptions were communist party newspapers such as the French *L'Humanité*). Bulgarian-language broadcasts on short wave by the BBC, the Voice of America and Radio Free Europe were jammed. Even so, many people were able to tune in and listen to these stations because the jamming could not cover all frequencies and the whole territory of the country.

In the 1980s this form of total control gradually began to relax. Western music, films, books and fashion became more and more common. Nevertheless, when *perestroika* and *glasnost* were initiated in the Soviet Union, the Bulgarian leadership refused to grant the same rights to the local media. What years before had been the safest move for a Bulgarian editor – to reprint an article from a Soviet newspaper – was not at all encouraged in the case of iconoclastic, *glasnost*-era Soviet writings. The Bulgarian Communist Party leader, Todor Zhivkov, still attempted to hold on to the existing regime, arguing that Bulgaria had had *glasnost* and *perestroika* since 1956 – that is, since his rise to power.

In 1960, Bulgaria had 12 daily newspapers. By 1989, their number had barely increased, to 17.[7] These papers did not offer a variety of good reading. As a prominent Bulgarian writer and historian puts it succinctly, they were all one and the same: 'concrete uniformity, censored boredom, information deficiency, if not disinformation'.[8] Most of the time these newspapers had four pages in a broadsheet format and published exclusively information supplied by the leadership of the communist party and the official news agency. All these dailies were 'organs' of some party or state institution – the Central Committee of the Bulgarian Communist Party, the Fatherland Union, the Bulgarian Agrarian National Union, the Central Council of the Bulgarian Trade Unions, the Armed Forces, and so on.

By far the largest and most important daily was the publication of the Central Committee of the Bulgarian Communist Party, *Rabotnichesko Delo* (Workers' Cause). It was the mouthpiece of the party leadership, and functioned as the agenda- and tone-setter for all other mass media. The newspaper's circulation was disproportionately high – close to one million copies – primarily because communist party members were obliged to subscribe to it. All important emphases and changes of the party line were announced in *Rabotnichesko Delo*.

Newspapers were cheap and people would often buy several of them to look for an occasional interesting piece and to compare what different papers wrote, in an effort to find out at least a part of the truth. People would even stand in line for some newspapers and magazines: mostly special interest publications for sports, science and technology, arts and letters and entertainment.

There was practically no underground press. Ironically, the first 'dissident' publications were official Soviet ones from 1985 onwards. People lined up to buy *Moskovskie novosti*, *Ogonek* and *Sputnik* and avidly consumed the reading that had been denied to them for decades. For the first time, Bulgarian communist party leaders discovered that the Soviet press could be as dangerous to the established order as that of the West.

Until 1989, Bulgaria had only two state television channels. There was also one 'foreign' channel of Soviet television whose programmes were re-broadcast in the country. State radio had three main channels – Horizont, Hristo Botev and Orphei (on FM). There were also a number of regional radio and television centres. All of these were under the close control of the party–state. The majority of the television programmes were produced in Bulgaria, the Soviet Union or other countries of the Soviet bloc. Only in the 1980s were the rules relaxed and some Western programming allowed.

The 'import' and 'export' of news was divided between the two state news agencies – the Bulgarian Telegraph Agency (BTA) and Sofia Press. The former was the official provider (and gatekeeper) of world news to all mass media in the country while the latter had the important mission of creating a favourable image of Bulgaria abroad.

## Mass Media and Political Transition

A number of researchers have argued that the mass media have played a decisive role in the breakdown of the former Soviet bloc and in the transition processes in the individual countries. This certainly is true to a great extent for Bulgaria, and especially for the initial stages of the transformation. However, to some extent this is an over-simplification; reality has been, as might be expected, much more complex. The mass media, society and politics have interacted in these past six years in a way that is far from straightforward. It is difficult, if not impossible, to separate cause from effect in this turbulent environment. What we have witnessed in the years since late 1989 has been a complicated maze of effects and feedback that should be analysed cautiously against the background of all political, economic, social, psychological and cultural prerequisites and developments in Bulgaria.

The first democratic right regained by Bulgarians in the late autumn of 1989 – freedom of speech – was soon followed by another long-awaited one – freedom of the press. Moreover, print media became the fastest developing business after the party–state started loosening its grip on power. The deluge of new titles became one of the most important characteristics of the times; to the general euphoria it added the notion that not only could anyone buy any kind of newspaper, but also that one could publish one's own.

The first wave of new publications that emerged was those connected to the various political parties. On 1 February 1990, the restored Bulgarian Social Democratic Party started publishing again its daily *Svoboden Narod* ('Free Nation').[9] Only days later, on 12 February, the Union of Democratic Forces launched its own daily named *Demokratsia* ('Democracy'). *Demokratsia* soon became one of the two leading political party newspapers, the other being *Duma* ('Word') – the renamed *Rabotnichesko Delo*, now published by the Socialist (former Communist) Party. Greeted enthusiastically by a great number of readers, the new papers were followed by other publications of various political parties.

In mid-1990 what is generally considered the first independent newspaper came into existence – the privately-owned weekly *Reporter 7*. According to other researchers, however, the first private newspaper was a publication entitled *Businessman*, first established by a group of journalists in April 1990.[10] The year 1990 also witnessed the formation of the first private press groups. Notably, some of these were started by former journalists from the communist party organ, *Rabotnichesko Delo*. What was later to become the largest press group – 168 Chasa – began in April with a weekly for 'business, politics and show', named after the organization.

The press boom continued with special interest, tabloid, pornographic and erotic publications, or combinations of these. Gossip and nudity turned out to be very marketable. Ironically, the first publication to break up the long-held taboo on sexually implicit or explicit pictures was *Patriot* – a weekly newspaper formerly entitled *Civil Defence* and published by the paramilitary Organization for Support of the Defence. On the first page of its fourth issue dated 25 January 1990, *Patriot* published a colour photograph of four naked women surrounding a white horse. In an interview, the editor of *Patriot* said that the publisher had cut the subsidies to the paper, and its first three issues were not selling: a way out of the crisis had to be found.[11] The approach worked instantly and was used successfully afterwards by many editors and publishers.

The mushrooming of new publications went on throughout the next few years. According to official data,[12] 928 newspapers and 777 magazines were being published in Bulgaria in 1993 – quite an impressive number for a country with a population of only some 8.5 million. The actual figures may even be greater, as there is no central registration of print media and the lists used by the Institute of Statistics are probably incomplete. It seems that currently the print media market as a whole has reached the point of saturation under the specific circumstances. New titles have been appearing but now at a much slower pace. A large number of publications have folded, some after publishing only a single issue. Still, there seems to be a number of niches that have not yet been completely filled.

**Trends in Press Development in the Post-Communist Period**

The beginning of this press pluralization was marked by the proliferation of newspapers published by newly formed or resurrected political parties, groups and movements. This was only natural after decades of living in a totalitarian system where diversity of political parties and opinions was not allowed. In the highly politicized atmosphere of the early transition period, people were seeking and avidly reading papers that were offering a striking departure from the dull, uniform press under communist rule.

As time went by, however, the initial interest in the party press began to fade. Since 1991, the circulation of the leading political newspapers has been steadily and dramatically declining. The average circulation of *Duma* went from 680,000 copies in 1990 to 70,000 in 1995; in the same period, the circulation of *Demokratsia* shrank from 420,000 to 50,000.[13] The numerous splits experienced by a number of political parties contributed to the fragmentation of the audience, leading in turn to the marginalization of some publications and the folding of others. There are several main reasons for the gradual decline of the partisan press. Faced with enormous economic hardships, sky-rocketing prices, growing unemployment and thriving crime, people grew disappointed with the speed, and probably the direction, of the transition.

Of course, all problems were blamed on the inability of the politicians to cope with the crisis, and on their corruption. As a result, large masses of people started losing interest in politics and consequently in reading the party-owned press. The second reason seems to be the fact that most party newspapers did not live up to the expectation of becoming professionally-run publications that provided objective information to their readers. Opinion journalism was predominant, attacks on political opponents were common, often ungrounded and expressed in crude language. The third reason is purely economic: as people grew poorer, newspapers became more expensive, and fewer readers could afford to buy several different publications, as they did previously.

The new press formed in three distinct ways. First, most of the existing publications changed their old compromised names and removed from their front pages the graphic symbols from the totalitarian past. Second, a number of papers and magazines were able to get rid of their former owners – usually various political, government or trade organizations – and became more or less independent. Third, new or in some cases resurrected publications which had existed before communist rule were established. The most notable example of the first type is *Rabotnichesko Delo*, which changed its name to *Duma* and now identifies itself as a 'daily of the Bulgarian Socialist Party'.

The second route has involved much legal ambiguity concerning ownership and copyright. Generally, the mechanism for establishing the independence of a publication would be a request for independence put forward by the editorial employees of a publication. As permission was usually not granted initially (no one would, for instance, part voluntarily with a profit-making newspaper), strikes or other forms of protest would follow. This approach worked, for example, with *Sturshel* ('Gadfly'), the former Bulgarian Communist Party's weekly newspaper for humour and satire. Another profit-making publication – *Orbita* (Orbit), a weekly paper for popular science and technology, published by the Communist Youth League – also managed to break free but had to change its name to *Nova Orbita* (New Orbit) and was left with practically no assets whatsoever.

Such an approach would clearly be unthinkable in countries with fundamental legal codes. Under the communist system, however, authoritarianism and state socialism obviated the need for an elaborate legal definition of media ownership and copyright standards. Publishing institutions could be said to exist only to the extent that they would pocket the profits of the publication or cover its losses. These legal ambiguities, and probably the feelings of journalists that they were entitled to their compensation after decades of totalitarian control, facilitated the process of press independence.

Yet the manner in which *Orbita* and some other publications underwent their change of status could hardly be defined as privatization. The only real thing that journalists from this paper managed to privatize was their own expertise. Much more consequential was the large-scale privatization of publications such as *Troud* ('Labour'), the daily of the old-regime trade unions, and *Duma* of the Socialist Party. The former has now grown into one of the largest and most successful publishing groups, now named Media Holding. Two Bulgarian researchers explain the process in the following way:

> The rapid privatization of print media could be seen as a preemptive defence against expected retributive legislation punishing old-regime

organizations (the communist party, the communist youth organization, the Agrarian Union, trade unions, the Fatherland Front) which issued the six major dailies and a number of other magazines. The law on confiscation of the property of these organizations was passed by the parliament in December 1991, but by then practically all the major political organizations that existed under the communist regime had transferred their property rights to newly established, legally independent publishing firms. Not all of the new editions survived the changes, but when entering the competitive market all of them relied on the assets of their precursors.[14]

Another important trend was set off by the formation of a limited number of powerful new press groups whose sources of capital are not exactly known. By far the most successful of these has been the 168 Chasa Press Group founded in 1990 by former journalists from *Rabotnichesko Delo*. The group made a start in April 1990 with the weekly *168 Chasa* ('168 Hours') and expanded a year later with a national, tabloid-format daily, *24 Chasa*. The latter quickly became the most popular newspaper, with a circulation hovering at about 300,000, currently about 270,000.

Such favourable developments encouraged the group to acquire other publications as well as starting new ones, although not all of these were a success. An evening paper, *Vrabets* ('Sparrow'), which began a year after *24 Chasa*, had to be discontinued. At least one other venture was a failure, involving a well-known daily published until 1989 under the name *Otechestven Front* ('Fatherland Front'). After the fall of communism, the paper was renamed *Otechestven Vestnik* ('Fatherland Gazette'). Never reaching a high circulation, it went bankrupt and was purchased by the 168 Chasa Press Group in 1994. An expensive advertising campaign was launched to mark the 'revival' of the daily under its original name *Otechestven Front*. The resurrected paper, however, had a very brief life and folded on 1 June 1995.

*Standart*, launched in August 1992, marked the appearance of another significant publishing company started by the powerful business group Tron. The daily has performed reasonably well – it gradually expanded from eight to 64 tabloid-size pages, has a special Sunday edition, and currently enjoys an average circulation of about 80,000.[15] Media Holding, the privatized trade union publishing house, has also been rapidly expanding and is now the most serious competitor to the 168 Chasa Press Group. In addition to its daily *Troud*, Media Holding now publishes, among other papers, a weekend edition and also an evening spin-off called *Noshten Troud* ('Nightly Labour'), both of them quite successful. The company also acquired and tried to revive a one-time popular magazine named *Cosmos*, but quickly abandoned this.

## Press Economics in a Nutshell

When the barriers to press freedom were raised in early 1990, the market was hungry for new publications; they appeared in an explosive manner, quickly filling this void. At that point, people longed to buy a significant number of newspapers and magazines and could generally afford to do so. This potential, however, could not be fully exploited, as there still was no free market in place, creating bottlenecks. The state still controlled the paper supply, printing and distribution. Many publications wanted to raise their circulation but were prevented by the shortage of newsprint. Moreover, the government could exercise control by allocating paper to its preferred publications. During the round-table negotiations in 1990, for example, it was agreed that political party newspapers would be preferentially supplied with newsprint. In the same year, the government reduced the quantity of paper for some of the most popular special interest titles by 22 per cent.[16]

In 1991, the price of paper also increased drastically – by about 20 times – and printing costs rose steeply. This hit a great number of publications very hard, especially smaller and more independent ones that did not have the backing of political parties or powerful business groups. Many newspapers and magazines had to fold, while others tried to cope with the crisis by reducing their frequency, number of pages per issue or circulation. The printing plants and the centralized distribution system, owned by the state, enjoyed monopoly positions in the market and could be used as powerful instruments for government control of the press. Printing plants were able to set their own prices, change the priority order of printing and delay (or even completely refuse) the production of individual publications. Press Distribution, the state-owned enterprise, also had no competitors and could set the terms of the contracts. It determined the commission percentage, the number of copies it would take for news-stand sale and even the maximum number of subscriptions per publication. Newspapers and magazines were not distributed within the cities and around the country according to the differing demands; instead, they were delivered to the most convenient news-stands so as to minimize transport and other expenses. As a result, the number of copies was insufficient in some outlets while in others there were more than needed. Finally, publishers were in practice unable to keep track of the actual number of copies sold and the breakdown of the sales.

This situation not only made life difficult for an enormous number of publications: publishers often voiced their concern that the state monopoly on printing and distribution was actually used by the government to favour some friendly newspapers while making life difficult for others. Looking for a way out, larger publishing groups started their own distribution networks, and a number of private distribution companies also appeared. Privately-owned printing plants have been slower to appear because of the large investments required but this process also is under way. The 168 Chasa Press Group, for example, only recently inaugurated its new, modern printing plant.

While the newspaper market has been quite lively, magazines have generally not fared well. One obvious reason is that the high-quality paper and printing required for magazines have made them too expensive for the average customer. According to a recent survey done by the Bulgarian subsidiary of Gallup, each of the top six magazines in the country commands on a regular basis only between one and four per cent of the audience.[17] Attempts to start a weekly magazine of the *Time* or *Newsweek* type have not been successful so far. The market is populated mostly by women's titles, one male-oriented magazine of the *Playboy* kind, and a number of other erotic or outright pornographic publications.[18] The taxation of the print media has also generated a lot of controversy.

Voices have often been raised asking for lower taxes for 'serious' publications while placing a bigger burden on erotic and pornographic ones. While this has not been enacted, the government did introduce, effective from 1 April 1994, a value-added tax (VAT) of 18 per cent which applied to all activities associated with print media, including advertising. The VAT was called a 'killer tax' and was vehemently attacked by publishers even before it went into effect. On 28 March 1994, all major newspapers stopped publishing to protest against the tax, and a number of private radio stations joined the strike. In response, the minister of finances said in public that Bulgarians would be better off without the papers. In spite of the heavy tax burden, most publications survived, though it represented a significant blow to the press.

Advertising has been slow to develop as a major source of income for the Bulgarian print media, and the main reason for this has nothing to do with the press itself. In a distressed economy where short supply of goods and rapidly rising prices later on have been the rule, advertising has not been the top priority. This has been gradually changing, however, and advertising is becoming a growing business and an increasingly important source of revenue for the printed media.

Unlike other countries of the former Soviet bloc, where foreign investments have been significant, the Bulgarian print media are mostly locally owned. Still, there are a limited number of publications with foreign participation. The first one – *Computerworld* – was started in early 1991 and is a joint venture of IDG Communications with Bulgarian partners.[19] Another moderately successful paper is the weekly *Cash* – a partnership of the Ringier media company.

*Press Law*

Paradoxically enough (although typical of Bulgaria) the 1990 press boom took place not as a result of favourable new regulations, but rather in spite of the still operative communist legal codes. At that time there had been no form of legal change in this area. Still, the communist party had relaxed some of the regulations, and the agreements reached at the round-table talks also gave a boost to the print media explosion.

The initial euphoria caused by the newly-gained press freedom was soon replaced by different moods within society. Many became irritated at the openly partisan content of party-affiliated newspapers, the shortage of information in them, and the lack of a civilized dialogue among political forces. Others were dissatisfied with the proliferation and open dissemination of erotic and pornographic publications. This group of discontented citizens was joined by publishers of 'serious' newspapers who felt that they should not be treated on an equal basis with the 'indecent' tabloid press. They began to press for some form of regulation, imposing limitations on erotic and pornographic publications – in the form of either higher taxes or state-controlled means of distribution and sales.

It was probably these feelings, as well as the desire to protect the fledgling freedom of the press, that in 1991 brought about a set of draft proposals on a new media law. One version was the Law on Mass Information Activities, drafted by the Secretariat of the Union of Bulgarian Journalists.[20] This aimed to regulate the obtaining, processing and dissemination of information 'via newspapers, magazines, newsletters, radio, television, cinema, and any other means making the information available to an indefinite number of people'. Although the objective of this law was to provide legal guarantees for the freedom of speech and of the press, it contained a number of vague statements, inconsistencies and obvious internal contradictions that could undermine its noble goal. For example, its first, undisputed principle of 'freedom and independence of information activities' was followed by the rather vague 'intolerability of publications and programmes of an amoral, destructive and libellous character'. Manifestly, these three terms – amoral, destructive and libellous – may be subject to different interpretations, and the latter two very much resemble the phraseology used by the communist party in the not-too-distant past.

The observance of these two and five other fundamental principles of mass information activities was to be controlled by a National Control Council. The 30-member council would include an equal number of representatives from parliament, the government, the judicial branch, trade unions and the Union of Bulgarian Journalists. However, the draft did not make clear how exactly this council was to execute its controlling functions.

The draft law made it mandatory for mass media to publish or broadcast free of charge all 'official announcements' of the government. Mass media were also required, under certain conditions, to give the right of response to people whose activities had been discussed in previous publications or broadcasts. It allowed print or broadcast media to be banned temporarily or permanently if they violated the stipulations of the law.

A second draft law was proposed by a commission at the Journalists' Initiative Club, based on a draft press law discussed in the Supreme Soviet of the Soviet Union.[21] This draft demonstrated more enthusiasm than experience and clear thinking. It mirrored some of the stipulations of the draft proposed by the Union of Bulgarian Journalists, namely the publishing of government announcements without charge and the right of response to published or broadcast stories. None of these drafts ever reached the stage of discussion in parliament, however. The press law issue was almost forgotten until April 1995 when Mr Hacho Boyadjiev, Director-General of Bulgarian National Television, introduced in parliament two new drafts – one on the state-owned Bulgarian National Television and Radio, and one on 'the freedom of speech and mass media'.[22] The latter, dealing to a great extent with the press, was sharply criticized by the two largest newspaper trusts, the 168 Chasa Press Group and Media Holding.

The main motive behind the criticism seems to have been the presence of anti-trust provisions in the draft, hurting the interests of powerful business groups. The law does not allow, for example, cross-ownership of print media and radio and television stations. Furthermore, according to the draft publishers may not own more than one daily. If the law were passed, the largest media trusts would have to sell or stop publishing many of their titles.[23] Whether as a result of this criticism or following behind-the-scenes pressure, the draft law on the freedom of speech and mass media was quickly withdrawn.[24]

Although the attitudes of journalists have little direct effect on media legislation, they are worth noting. According to unpublished data of the Union of Bulgarian Journalists, in 1990 the overwhelming majority of Bulgarian journalists favoured a law on the press. Nowadays, such a law is considered by most as a restriction on their freedom. The causes of this evolution are difficult to analyse but one explanation seems plausible. After the 1989 revolutions in Eastern Europe, the freedom of speech and of the press probably seemed to Bulgarian journalists too fragile unless backed up by legal guarantees. Also, little was known about media law in Western Europe and the United States. Five years of freedom (though not perfect) without a press law, combined with a flow of information and experts from the West (mainly the United States), have probably contributed to the currently prevalent attitudes of journalists in Bulgaria.

Legislators have mixed feelings.[25] Some say there is no need for a press law; others favour a law that would protect journalists and at the same time prevent them from abusing their alleged power, publishing unfounded allegations, outright lies and pornography, using foul language, and so on. Nevertheless, at the time of writing (late 1995), there remains no law on the press. Anyone may start a private newspaper or magazine as long as he or she has a formally registered company. The only legal regulations covering printed media come from the general provisions of the constitution, from the copyright law of 1993 and from the libel, insult and defamation provisions of the penal code.

## Major Players in the Bulgarian Media

Throughout the past three years, *24 Chasa*, published by the 168 Chasa Press Group, has managed to remain the largest-circulation daily in the country. It is widely read because of its numerous, brief and easily-digested pieces written in colloquial, often vulgar language. Additional advantages of the paper are its convenient (especially for reading in public transport) tabloid format, and its alleged independence of political parties. This most successful national daily, however, is often sneered at, especially by the intelligentsia. Many readers are turned off by its crude language and tabloid-leaning journalism with sloppy fact-checking.

The runner-up in mid-1995 was the daily *Troud*, owned by Media Holding. In late July of that year its circulation exceeded 150,000.[26] With its aggressive but well-considered strategy, Media Holding is the most serious and closest challenger to the leadership of the 168 Chasa Press Group. Third in the race of the dailies comes *Standart*, of the Tron group, with an average circulation of 80,000, reaching at times close to 100,000.[27] Although in tabloid format (like its two bigger competitors), this newspaper stands out for the light-blue paper on which it is printed, and for its commitment to a more balanced coverage and objective tone. The two major party-affiliated dailies – *Duma* and *Demokratsia* – have been going through recent crises due to their waning readerships and to internal struggles within their publishing companies, the BSP and the UDF. Their circulations are said to be around 70,000 and 50,000, respectively.

At a recent BSP conference, the editor of *Duma*, Stefan Prodev, accused the party leadership of manipulating the paper and of dubious business transactions. For the first time, the general public learned that an unknown businessman owned 49 per cent of the shares of the publishing house, Duma Press.

*Demokratsia* is also going through turmoil, with its editor-in-chief changed several times. By mid-summer 1995, it was announced that the newspaper would no longer be a publication of the UDF but a 'national daily'. Its publisher, the Demokratsia Agency, is to be transformed into a joint-stock company with 51 per cent of the shares to be held by the UDF. Another national daily, *Continent*, maintains a relatively low circulation of 20,000, while aiming at a more upward sector of the market. To be able to survive, however, it has been forced to run sweepstakes in order to attract readers. Such strategies, long known in the West, are becoming increasingly popular in Bulgaria. In addition to these and other general-interest titles, there are a great number of special-interest publications. A formerly non-existent niche – that of business-oriented newspapers – appeared with the gradual development of a free market. The *168 Chasa* weekly was the first serious entrant in this niche, although business topics accounted for only a part of its editorial content. The first business daily – *Pari* ('Money') – made its appearance on 14 May 1991,[28] and is still in publication. Like the *Financial Times*, this paper is printed on pink paper but is in tabloid format and has fewer pages than its British counterpart. Worth noting also are two financial weeklies – *Banker* and the more recent *Capital Press*.

In contrast with the years of totalitarianism and its grey uniformity of the press, the market nowadays is overpopulated with a variety of publications devoted to sports, entertainment, humour and satire, religion, health, automotive, paranormal and supernatural phenomena, youth subcultures, and the like. Titles have ranged from *Work Abroad* (featuring international job announcements) to *Oracle* ('transcendental issues') to *1001 Beer Mugs* ('organ' of the Beer Party) to such bad-taste publications as *The Shot-Down Condom*. Intellectual titles that once enjoyed a significant popularity have lost readership and have been forced to look for sponsors in order to survive.

**The Broadcast Media**[29]

The state-owned Bulgarian National Television and Radio have enjoyed great popularity during the years of transition. They have played an essential role in the democratic changes in the country by voicing diverse opinions, giving the floor to prominent politicians and opinion leaders of various orientations, and reporting or airing live the round-table negotiations and discussions in parliament. Significant coverage was also given to the revolutions in other East European countries. Such symbolic events as the fall of the Berlin Wall and the bloody demonstration in Bucharest (Romania), were shown on television and followed by large audiences.

Acknowledging the great impact of these media, politicians have consequently been fighting perpetual wars to gain control over them. Each new parliamentary majority has invariably replaced the heads of Bulgarian

National Television, Bulgarian National Radio and the Bulgarian Telegraph Agency. Battles have also been in progress over media law, private broadcasting and cable television – all these issues heavily involving political as well as financial interests.

After the fall of communism, the licensing of private television and radio stations became an important and controversial issue. Broadcasting is still regulated by the communications law of 1975. Of course, this law from the era of totalitarian rule does not provide for private radio and television, but in spite of this unfavourable legal background, progress was made in the form of a loophole in the law which allows experimental broadcasting on frequencies other than those of the officially existing stations.[30]

It is through this loophole, for example, that VOA–Europe came to Bulgaria. In 1991 the Washington-based International Media Fund donated through the Open Society Fund–Sofia[31] studio equipment valued at $132,000. The equipment was intended for the Vitosha radio station, started by the Applied Research and Communications (ARC) Fund at the Center for the Study of Democracy, Sofia. Vitosha radio went on the air in January 1992 in the FM band, formally as experimental broadcasting.[32] Initially it broadcast the English-language programmes of VOA–Europe with a small portion of original Bulgarian programming that was gradually expanded. By July 1995, Vitosha radio planned to air only local programming of its own.[33] After VOA–Europe came the BBC, Deutsche Welle and France Inter – each of them broadcasting in its original language on FM. In the area of television, the first foreign television channel to move into Bulgaria after the fall of communism was the French Television 5, whose programme was retransmitted by Bulgarian Television.

The legalization and development of private broadcasting turned out to be a difficult process. There was a significant pressure on the government and on parliament to allow private radio and television channels, yet at the same time there was no law to provide for this. As a result, the Parliamentary Commission on Broadcasting took a provisional step, creating a Temporary Council on Radio Frequencies, Television Channels and Cable Networks to review applications and grant licences to private broadcasters.

The temporary council drafted a document[34] that set up rules, criteria and priorities for broadcast licensing, according to which licences for radio stations are valid for five years, and for television channels and cable networks ten years. The government Mail and Long-distance Communications Committee also issued its own document, entitled *A Brief Description of the Regulations for Starting Regional Broadcasting Stations*, which covers the technical side of the issue, primarily frequency and safety regulations.

On 25 June 1992, the temporary council licensed the first six private radio stations to broadcast on FM for the Sofia region. These were selected out of 24 applicants and then went through the procedures required by the Mail and Long-distance Communications Committee to obtain the necessary certificates. On 9 July 1992, the council issued some 30 more licences to private radio stations in the country. As of May 1995, there were 110 licensed radio stations in Bulgaria, 46 of which are active.[35]

The variety of television channels is much more limited. In addition to the two channels of the state-owned National Television and the Russian Ostankino programme, currently there are only two private channels – Nova Televizia ('New Television') and Televizia Sedem Dni ('Seven Days Television'). The former broadcasts from 10 or 10.30 a.m. to approximately midnight, while the latter has just begun experimental broadcasting for only a few hours per day. Their programming involves a heavy dose of soap operas.

The current situation regarding broadcasting law has once again proved an old Bulgarian saying that there is nothing more permanent than the temporary. The Temporary Council on Radio Frequencies, Television Channels and Cable Networks remains in existence. The temporary statute of Bulgarian National Television and of Bulgarian National Radio, approved by parliament in 1990 and insignificantly modified in 1993, was only recently challenged by the constitutional court. Although the 1991 constitution requires a broadcasting law, not a single draft has managed to reach the voting stage in three successive parliaments.

At the time of writing, three new drafts have been submitted – by the BSP, by the UDF, and by the Director-General of Bulgarian National Television. The draft of the Socialists[36] and that of the opposition[37] share the same title and a number of provisions. Both of them cover state-owned and private radio and television, and also cable networks. Both drafts propose the creation of a National Council on Radio and Television as an independent executive body.

In the BSP law the National Council has nine members, six of whom are to be elected by parliament, while the president, the prime minister, and the higher judicial council each have the right to appoint one member. The UDF law envisages 13 members: nine elected by parliament, and two appointed by the president and two more by the Council of Ministers. There is one more subtle difference: in the latter draft, five of the nine members elected by the parliament come from the majority and four from the opposition; in the former (the socialist draft), there is no similar requirement, and this gives the parliamentary majority the opportunity (if only in theory) to elect only persons whom it favours.

The opposition draft bans former and present employees of the state security services from being members of the National Council on Radio and Television, while in the other draft the ban holds only for present employees. This seemingly small difference touches a very sensitive point because of the legacy of the KGB-style security institutions in Bulgaria: their former employees are alleged to be still playing an important role in the political and business life of the country.

The UDF draft provides for an additional 33-member advisory body, elected by parliament; this 'national public council' will be charged with monitoring whether the programming of Bulgarian National Radio and Television conforms to the provisions of the law. The council is intended to act as a freedom-of-speech watchdog.

The state-owned radio and television, according to both laws, are to be funded by the state budget, with further income derived from advertising, their own business activities and sponsorship. There are additional provisions to regulate advertising, sponsorship, the access of government officials and political groups to air time, and other issues. In both drafts, the licensing of private broadcast media is to be carried out by the National Council on Radio and Television. Political parties and advertising agencies may not apply for licences, and an applicant's foreign financial share may not exceed 49 per cent.

The lack of a broadcasting law, the activities of the Parliamentary Commission on Broadcasting and the latest draft laws have provoked heated discussions in the mass media. The arguments have been to a great extent motivated by the significant political and financial stakes behind the long-overdue legislation. So far, no consensus has been reached and it can hardly be expected soon in the highly polarized Bulgarian political space. In the meantime, there have been indications that the government's Mail and Long-distance Communications Committee is trying to take power away from the Temporary Council on Radio Frequencies, Television Channels and Cable Networks and take over the licensing of private broadcasting media and cable networks.[38] If this occurs, private broadcasting may fall under the direct control of the government.[39]

## The Media Transition: Future Prospects

It is a formidable task to summarize and analyse what has developed with Bulgarian mass media from late 1989 to mid-1995. Still more difficult at this stage is to make predictions of their future development because of the continuing turbulent course of events. As this review was being finished, the war for control over the national media continued, with new developments regularly occurring.

On 23 June 1995, the Socialist majority in parliament voted to elect new heads of national television, radio and BTA. The former directors-general of television and of radio were sacked, and the director of BTA had recently died. The 42-year-old Ivan Granitski, a journalist and Marxist philosopher, became the new head of national television. His appointment drew the heaviest fire from the opposition, as he is a member of the BSP and had recently served as the head of its organization in the capital. Granitski was also criticized for not having experience in television. This development was characterized by many non-Socialist politicians as further tightening of the control over the national media.

What also angered many was the way the parliamentary majority imposed its will: the BSP proposed only one candidate for each position with no alternatives. All moves by the opposition to bring in the incumbent directors and the candidates to be interviewed by MPs before the voting were blocked by the majority. The opposition had absolutely no way of countering the Socialists' moves in parliament. One of its few possible formal reactions was to approach the constitutional court, which is allegedly sympathetic to the UDF.

In September 1995, that court declared a number of texts in the temporary statute of Bulgarian National Television and of Bulgarian National Radio to be repugnant to the Constitution, and this decision removes a number of powers from the parliamentary commission on television, radio and the BTA: to approve the structure and the regulations governing the work of the national media; to endorse their ruling bodies and budgets; to have a say in programming; and to hold periodic hearings of the directors-general. A spokesman for the constitutional court explained that from that moment on, the activities of the commission would be limited only to working out a draft media law.[40]

This decision follows a heated discussion over the statute of the commission on television, radio and the BTA and over parliamentary control of the national media in general. One of most frequently heard arguments was that the procedures have so far violated the principle of separation of powers. Instead of being a strictly legislative body, critics said, parliament and its commission were also exercising close executive control over the national media. For its part, the Socialist majority has accused UDF supporters of having lived with the temporary statute of these media for five years, and acting against it only now when it hurt their political interests.

In order to regain legal control of national media, the parliamentary majority may either try to vote in a revised statute in place of the overturned one, or finally to pass the long-overdue media law. It seems reasonable to expect the latter, as Socialists now have a sufficient majority in parliament to vote any law they consider acceptable. Under the current distribution of power, the opposition can do little but hope for a presidential veto or a constitutional court ruling against what they view as unfavourable laws.

Clearly, the media war is far from over and it will most probably be fought again under a different majority in a future parliament. It has been an important part of the transition period in Bulgaria; in the absence of viable alternative private television, the National Television service has been one of the most influential media in the country. Consequently, it has been a prime target for all politicians. National Radio has also been an influential and quite trusted medium, still holding the greatest share of the radio audience. Private stations, however, are gaining in popularity, some of them with ambitions to become national in their broadcasting scope. Moreover, because of the political pressure on the National Radio station and the frequent turnover among executives, a number of able journalists have left it and have moved to these private stations. This contributes to the shift of audiences and influence away from the state-run radio. Finally, cable television, while it does exist, still remains a mostly illegal business. Few licences have been granted, and the only one for a national cable operator has already been revoked. These problems have emerged not so much from political issues as from the significant financial stakes involved.

Newspapers today, and especially the party-affiliated ones, have to a great extent lost the extraordinary appeal they had in the early 1990s. The impoverishment of Bulgarians and their disenchantment have both had their effect, and the press itself has not done much to improve its standing. Pursuing quick financial success, many publications have resorted to gossip, scandal, unchecked sensational facts, personal attacks, erotica and pornography. The rapidly expanding number of publications in the early 1990s left the market with a shortage of experienced, professional journalists, and this takes its toll on the quality of the published materials. Against the background of the slow economic, social and socio-psychological changes in the country, it is hardly to be expected that printed media will take a quick turn for the better.

The final question is whether post-communist Bulgarian media had a real impact on society. At least for the first two years after the fall of the communism, the answer is a definite 'yes'. At that time, the media were riding the crest of the social wave and were generally giving the public what it had longed for under communist rule. Later on, when the high political polarization and party-commitment began to fade, a number of media (especially newspapers) failed to adapt to the new situation. At that point, they in effect stopped playing a leadership role. It is not likely that they will regain this role, as it seems typical for the media only in periods of crisis and sudden dramatic changes. In the years to come, politics and ideology will probably play a less important role in the development of the mass media. As the new capitalists come to the fore, the field will be affected increasingly by financial interests. Still, it is unlikely that both politicians and business people will completely ignore the propaganda and public relations functions of the media, and will therefore seek to use the media and related political instruments to reinforce their control.

## NOTES

1. State-owned media are Bulgarian National Television, Bulgarian National Radio, the Bulgarian Telegraph (News) Agency, or BTA, and regional radio and television stations.
2. Bulgarian Telegraph Agency (BTA), *Vatreshna Informatsia*, 13 Sept. 1995.
3. *Standart News*, 14 Sept. 1995.
4. *Continent*, 14 Sept. 1995.
5. *24 Chasa*, 14 Sept. 1995.
6. This and other observations come from my personal experience as a journalist and also as an active participant in the transition to free press in Bulgaria.
7. *Statistical Yearbook* (Sofia: Institute of Statistics 1994).
8. V. Mutafchieva, *Continent*, 2–3 March 1995.
9. In fact, *Svoboden Narod* started as a weekly and in May became a daily; in November 1991 it reverted to a weekly frequency.
10. M. Velinova, *1000 Vestnika* (Sofia: Department of Journalism and Mass Communication, Sofia University 1994).
11. Ibid.
12. *Statistical Yearbook*, op. cit.
13. *168 Chasa*, 31 July–6 Aug. 1995.
14. R. Kolarova and D. Dimitrov, 'Postcommunist Media in Bulgaria', in <soc.culture.bulgaria>, 1995.
15. *168 Chasa*, 31 July–6 Aug. 1995.
16. M. Velinova, op. cit.
17. *24 Chasa*, 4 July 1995.
18. E. Dainov, personal communication, 1995.
19. M. Velinova, op. cit.
20. 'Zakon za masovata informatsionna deinost', *Pogled*, 24 June 1991.
21. 'Zakon za svobodata na informatsiata', 1991.
22. *Troud*, 25 April 1995.
23. *24 Chasa*, 25 April 1995; *Troud*, 25 April 1995.
24. *Standart*, 27 April 1995.
25. *Maritsa*, 9 March 1995.
26. *Troud*, 25 July 1995.
27. Ibid.
28. M. Velinova, op. cit.
29. The Bulgarian Telegraph Agency, though not a broadcast medium, has been included in this section as it is treated in the existing legislation together with National Radio and Television.
30. T. Tsvetanov, Legal Counsel of the Open Society Fund–Sofia, personal communication, 1992.
31. The Open Society Fund–Sofia is one of the foundations set up by the American financier George Soros throughout Central and Eastern Europe and in several other parts of the world.
32. T. Tsvetanov, op. cit.
33. P. Georgiev, former director of Vitosha Radio, personal communication, 1995.
34. This paper has a rather long title: *Conditions, Criteria and Priorities Used by the Temporary Council on Radio Frequencies, Television Channels and Cable Networks in Reviewing Requests for the Creation and Airing of Radio and Television Channels*. By contrast, its provisions are very few and quite brief.
35. R. Radev, presentation at the Conference on Freedom of Information and its Legal Regulation under the Conditions of Transition to Democracy, Sofia: 30–31 May 1995.
36. K. Marinova, 'Zakon za radioto i televiziata', 1995.

37. E. Mihailov, 'Zakon za radioto i televiziata', 1995.
38. *168 Chasa*, 22–8 May 1995; *Duma*, 23 May 1995.
39. *168 Chasa*, 10–16 April 1995.
40. BTA, 'Vatreshna informatsia', 19 Sept. 1995.

www.ingramcontent.com/pod-product-compliance
Ingram Content Group UK Ltd.
Pitfield, Milton Keynes, MK11 3LW, UK
UKHW020429010325
455677UK00029B/1064